# Fatherhood in 40-Minute Snapshots

## Jeremy G. Schneider

ISBN: 0999687506

ISBN 13: 9780999687505

Library of Congress Control Number: 2017919038

Two Okapis Productions, LLC, Baldwin, NY

*For my Sweetie:*
*It's amazing the life, and these two lives, we've created*
*together. Wouldn't want to ride this roller coaster of*
*Happy Chaos with anyone else.*

*For my Okapis:*
*My life changed so dramatically the day you were born that*
*I wouldn't be the man I am today without you both in my life. Here's to*
*another few decades of sharing great moments together.*

# Table of Contents

# Introduction

Almost every morning since my twins, Dorit and Lucas (or "okapis," as my wife and I call them, after the unique-looking animals only found in the Democratic Republic of the Congo. An okapi looks like a giant horse with zebra stripes on its hind legs and a giraffe-like tongue), were born, I've had to go to work. When they were young, I would sometimes leave before they were even awake. I do most of my writing during my morning train commute, after I've left my family, my foundation. On this forty-minute train ride, I think about what I'm doing right and what I need to work on. Some mornings I review research on parents—especially fathers—and write about ways parents can benefit from the insights shared in these studies. Some mornings my emotions are so raw from something that happened with my family that I need to write them down and work through them.

When I began writing these snapshots my children were not even two years old. I already believed that fathers were important. But I didn't truly understand just how valuable fathers are in the lives of their children until I started reviewing the research. On some level I understood that I had the power to make a difference in the lives of my children, but I didn't know how to focus that energy in the best way. I needed an Obi-Wan Kenobi to help me hone my Force. So, as a nearly lifelong student of psychology and a marriage and family therapist, I turned to what I knew: the studies and the literature on child-rearing.

Most of the studies on fatherhood are pretty conclusive—involved fathers make a huge difference in their children's lives in a number of different areas: school, social competence, relationships, and even future life satisfaction as adults. In fact, studies have shown that children of involved fathers are significantly more likely to do better in school, have higher IQs, be more socially competent, have healthier future relationships, and experience higher life satisfaction as adults.

What I took away from the research was that when it comes to father involvement, there are four important things to remember.

1) The quality of the time matters more than the quantity.
Even though I work outside the home, I have built a strong relationship with my children; I'm still involved with them. This has been particularly critical for me as my own father was an absentee father (he was always at work or working in the basement, leaving all of the child-rearing to my abusive mother). I know too well the lasting effects of his lack of involvement.

Building a strong relationship with my kids in limited time has not been easy, but it is absolutely possible. When it comes to father–child relationships, quantity is a myth. I was worried that if I didn't have a lot of time with my children, I might not be able to build a healthy relationship with them. But the reality is that any bonding time I have with them makes a difference. Plus, those bonding moments have a way of building momentum, leading to more bonding moments and more bonding opportunities.

2) Consider what "involvement" truly means.
I was pretty sure involvement was more than just having fun with my kids, but what else did it mean? Yes, having fun is important and necessary to build powerful bonds with our children, but we also have to meet their needs, be their caretaker. I have to show our children that I can be what they need, whether that means changing diapers, feeding them, putting them to bed, taking them to school, listening to their problems, etc. I need to do for them what they need me to do. This also includes disciplining them when they break my rules. This is what being involved in their lives and helping them to receive the benefits of my involvement means. When I meet my children's needs, they see me as being involved, as being present for them.

3) Involvement is not defined by the father, but by the child.
This was a more difficult concept for me to grasp. My children feel I'm involved, so I know my involvement has bestowed profound benefits. But

if I felt I was an involved father but my children didn't, the benefits of my involvement would be lost. Children have to feel and internalize their father's involvement, feel that bond, that sense of intimacy. This means I can never rest on my laurels, feeling I've done enough to be involved—because if my children don't feel connected to me, it doesn't matter how involved I think I am. At the end of each day, I ask myself, "Did I do enough to show my children how much I care about and love them?" This has helped me to be a better dad when I come home from a terrible day at the office. Regardless of my day, my kids still need me (even though on those bad days, I'm less patient and understanding). I don't need to perfect, but I do need to be what they need me to be—even if I don't feel I can do it on that day. And the truth is, when I really try to be there for them on those days, we often create a memory that can last a long time, like when it was cold out and they put each of their hands in my jacket sleeves (I'm pretty short and my sleeves are usually not) so we could hold hands together without getting cold.

4) The fundamentals of involvement do not change over time—even though how we relate to our children does.
My children are now fifteen years old, and our lives are constantly chang-ing. Certainly how they need me now is very different from how they needed me when they were babies and toddlers and preschoolers. But they still need me. And it's my job to figure out how I can meet their needs, to remain involved even though how they need me has changed so dramatically. When they were younger, it was easier to see how they needed me—food, diapers, etc.—but now the needs are more subtle. I help them deal with their emotions, with the challenges of school and the pressures they experience as young adults. I need to be able to relate to my children at their level. We connect by having fun, by talking about top-ics of mutual interest, and by sharing our lives, but I must still find ways to meet their needs.

Our children will never really stop needing us—they just start needing us in different ways. It's our job as parents to figure out how they need us and be there for them. This will ensure our involvement throughout their lives, and a connection that is both special and powerful.

Each piece you're about to read is a snapshot of my life as a parent. I hope these snapshots, which span more than a decade, help you work through any parenting issues you're thinking about, help you remember to enjoy parenting, help you feel connected with your children, and help you feel less alone as you deal with the challenges of parenting (because we all have parenting challenges!).

# Chapter One

# In the Beginning

*When my wife got pregnant, I realized that pregnancy is a built-in adjustment period, especially for us fathers. It's a time to acclimate ourselves to the idea of becoming a father. Even though I ended up having only seven months instead of the standard nine, this time was valuable in helping me get psychologically and physically ready. But I wish I had known more about the good things fatherhood entailed. I faced many emotional challenges in the early months of my children's lives.*

**What I Have Instead**

I fantasize about the life Gem and I would have if we were free to travel wherever we wanted. If we were free to go out to dinner, see a movie, and visit museums without feeling guilty for leaving, and worrying about who was watching our children. I fantasize about the time we would have to actually talk, share our lives, get to know each other all over again. I imagine we would be doing so many fun and interesting things together, rather than arguing over where to live and how to afford it while sending our kids to school. The stress of having children, trying to do what's best for them, providing for them, is a dominating force in our relationship. Becoming a parent really has changed everything, and there are times when I'm left wondering about all that I'm missing.

But life is about choices, about taking certain paths rather than standing at the fork unsure of what to do. There are certainly some benefits to a child-free life, but for me, they no longer outweigh the benefits of having children. This is often what prospective parents—especially men—have a difficult time understanding. Before and during Gem's pregnancy, all I could see was the cost of having children, the potential negative impact on our marriage and the lack of freedom it would inflict on our lives. This made it impossible to imagine why we would want to have children, or to imagine I could ever be ready for it. Gem, on the other hand, seemed to intuitively understand many of the positive aspects of having children from the very start.

All the negative stuff has come to pass, but since I've held my children in my arms and interacted with them, I have come to realize so many of the good things about having children. I would never go back—even if I could.

I can close my eyes and hear my children laugh. It's one of the most beautiful sounds I've ever heard, especially if they're laughing because of something I did. The sound is an expression of pure joy, unadulterated, unencumbered, unfiltered. It's so powerful that I feel joyous. I feel love— something I often lacked in my childhood experience.

I marvel at how much my children learn and grow on a daily basis. Watching them experience something for the first time is awe inspiring. The way they take in a new environment, absorb their surroundings and react to them, is thoroughly enjoyable. Watching how they integrate this new knowledge with other things they know is fascinating. Children's brains grow at such a rapid rate that it's a challenge for my wife and me to keep up. But it's a good kind of challenge, a fun and exciting one.

Their affection and love is like nothing I've ever known. When Dorit caresses my face, I almost always tear up. My heart swells when Lucas puts his hand on my shoulder while we're reading at bedtime. They are learning how to love from Gem and me; it's the best feeling in the world. I had no idea I could feel such intense joy, happiness, and love from being with my children. I didn't get that part—didn't understand and couldn't see how this was possible before they were born. I could see only the stress and overwhelming responsibility. I thought I would have to give and give and give. And I do. And I wouldn't have it any other way, because they give back so much, especially if I'm open to receiving.

I think about my wife, about how she is the most loving person I've ever known, about how she has worked so hard to be there for our children every single day, often by herself, without enough sleep. Though we have to work so hard to keep our relationship strong, I wouldn't want to share this experience with anyone else in the entire world. We are stronger because of our children, because they have made us bigger than ourselves. We are a family now—the loving, caring family we always wanted.

I used to try to envision my life with children and my stomach would get tense and upset. I would get anxious thinking of all I would lose, of all that I didn't know. But now I hear songs about divorce or watch shows where the father only sees his children every other weekend and it hurts—it genuinely causes me physical pain to think of being without my children. I can't envision my life without them. Being a father has become such a huge part of who I am. I may have given up a lot to take this path, but I have gained so much more.

## The Little Things

Parenting can be overwhelming and exhausting and draining—especially if I forget to pay attention to the special moments. When I remember to enjoy the moments of love and intimacy with my family, parenting is a lot more positive than I ever thought it could be. Here are some of the little joys I never expected.

**Watching them think:** Watching my children trying to formulate complicated sentences was one of the greatest experiences of my life. One night, my little boy was trying to tell me about something he remembered. He started stammering, in part because he was so excited to tell me and in part because he was trying to relay an event that happened quite some time ago—and time is an extraordinarily complicated concept for a three-year-old to grasp.

He tried it one way and stopped.

He tried it another way and stopped.

My wife and I didn't say a word. I smiled at him to encourage him to keep trying, to work it out. Inside, however, I was cringing. I felt an incredibly intense love for him, watching him struggle, knowing the thought was in his head but that he didn't yet have a language to express it. It was both painful and inspiring to watch.

Finally, after what seemed like a very long time (but probably wasn't), he got his point across. I was thankful he hadn't given up on himself. He needed me to let him work it out on his own. When he succeeded, the sense of pride was all his to enjoy. And my wife and I enjoyed our excitement over his ability to tell us what he was thinking.

**Hearing them talk:** When our twins first started talking, Gem and I loved listening to them talk to each other. Their conversations in the backseat of the car or in their room when they woke up in the morning gave me an incredible feeling of wonder. One of the first things they ever talked about was Jax—a game they made up and that involved making their toys talk to each other. Whoever woke up first would say, "Wanna play Jax?" For months they would play this game, and we had no idea what it was.

But as their language developed, so did their ability to converse with each other. They would console each other when they were scared or upset. "Lucas, you know Mommy always comes back," Dorit would say to calm him when they first started going to school. "Just think about your happy thoughts," one would say when the other would get scared at night. Or, "You can use my woobie tonight if you want." When Lucas couldn't find his woobie, Dorit would offer hers, and vice versa.

They would make each other laugh until they wore themselves out, and would also ask about each other's days—"What was your favorite part of the party?"—and look forward to hearing the answer.

Of course, they were children, and children aren't always nice to each other, but for the most part, listening to my children talk was one of my favorite privileges of being a parent. And still is. It's when I get to see how close they are, what they might be thinking, and how wonderful and intelligent they are.

**Watching them try to impress me**: I was often reminded of how important I was to my children when they would do things to impress me. Lucas would come running in to show me something he could do with a ball, or a new jump he had mastered; Dorit would show me a new dance step or try to demonstrate that she could juggle (which she couldn't). Most of these things were small to me but big to them—things they wanted me to see because my opinion mattered. But sometimes what they showed me was quite impressive, and I'd be delighted by how great it felt to see them do something so well.

**Experiencing their sweetness**: Sometimes my daughter would come out of nowhere and give me a kiss. Or my son would pat my back. They did things because they thought I might be sad or because they wanted me to know how they felt about me without saying anything. Receiving gestures of love and affection from my children was like nothing I'd ever experienced before. There was something so pure about it, so unselfish, so touching that I often felt like crying.

**Feeling how they felt about me**: The way Dorit would play with my sleeve while I was giving her her medication. The way she would play with my face when she sat on my lap, examining it as if trying to remember every freckle, wrinkle, hair, and mark. The way they called my name when they noticed I wasn't in the room with them. The way Lucas got so excited watching football with me because it was important to me: "I have to go watch football with Daddy now." There was no way I could have understood how these things would make me feel until I experienced them.

**Seeing their reactions when I came home**: The way they would run to the door yelling "DADDDEEEEE," especially after I'd had a rough day at the office, was delicious. They always gave me a hug and kiss, and usually tried to tell me something exciting that had happened to them that day. It was a lovely way to come home, and it always amazed me that I could mean that much to two little people.

Yes, parenting has been the hardest thing I've ever done in my life, and sometimes it can be so exhausting and overwhelming I just want to hide. But when I remember to notice the little moments, to bask in the good feelings they bring, the rest of it doesn't seem so hard at all.

**Expecting Fathers: Don't Expect an Immediate Connection**

I never expected to have children—mostly because I was terrified at the prospect of being a father. My friends and family didn't have any doubts about whether I would be a good father, but apparently I had enough anxiety for all of us.

Gem was so ready to have children that she had what I call "baby sense"; like well-trained spies who can track the people around them, my wife could close her eyes and tell me where each baby was, what it was wearing, and how old it was. I was happy if I saw the baby after she told me where it was. Before she got pregnant, her body was telling her it was time; mine was saying … nothing. When she got pregnant, she was excited and anxious. I was terrified.

During her pregnancy, Gem could feel a strong bond developing with our children, while I spent the first several months in shock. There was so much going on in her body, but for me, everything was the same. It wasn't until about the seven-month point that I began to feel like I'd be ready by the time they were born.

Our twins arrived almost ten weeks early, and when we had to go home without them, we were both distraught. We visited them in the hospital every day, but Gem felt as though a part of her were missing, that it was terribly wrong to not have them home. When I didn't feel that same sense of loss, I assumed it meant there was something wrong with me as a father. Maybe I shouldn't have had kids, as I'd feared all along.

The problem was that I didn't feel an immediate emotional connection with my children. How can you miss what you never had? I knew I loved them and would do anything I could to care for them. But I felt a strange emptiness, a blankness inside. I knew we were related, but they didn't feel like mine. They were strangers to me. I *knew* I loved them, but I didn't *feel* it. If I was a good father, I would've felt an immediate connection, right? This lack of connection was a sign I was failing as a father right off the bat—especially since their mother had such an obviously strong connection with them.

This disconnected feeling got worse because we had decided I would work and Gem would stay home with our babies. While she developed an even stronger relationship with our children at home, I spent more time away from them, making it that much harder to develop a connection. As the rest of my family got closer, I felt more and more distant from them.

On the subway home one day, a thought popped into my head: *Now I understand how fathers can leave their families after a baby is born.* What a jolt! I had expected a special connection, not to have sudden insight into fathers who leave their babies. What had I become? What had happened to me?

Most of what I felt in those first few months was fear, pressure, a sense of responsibility, and exhaustion—almost no warmth, love, or sense of closeness. I felt inadequate and even useless. I thought if I disappeared it wouldn't matter. The only reason I left work at a decent time was because I knew my wife needed my help. But I would still take the local subway home instead of the express, just to have a few extra minutes to myself. I had lost the closeness I previously enjoyed with my wife because she was so involved with our babies—making me feel more isolated and disconnected. Ironically, if we hadn't had twins, I think it would have been even worse. At least with two, I was always holding one, developing a connection without even realizing it, while Gem held the other.

I've since learned that many fathers have this experience but are afraid to talk about it. But by not talking about it, we create a sense of shame around the issue, as if there really is something wrong with a father (or a mother) who doesn't feel an immediate connection to his (or her) baby. I learned that I needed to remain involved and create opportunities for that connection with my children to develop.

What I didn't realize was that this connection often comes only with time. I needed to get to know my children and they needed to get to know me. While Gem experienced our babies' growing inside her for seven months, they only became a reality for me when they were born (and then they spent so much time at the hospital, so much time away from me). Within a few months, I felt something flutter in my chest when I looked at Dorit's face and it would it scrunch a certain way, or when Lucas heard a sound and would move his arms. Before I knew it, I felt such a strong connection I had trouble remembering what life was like when I didn't feel this way. That feeling only built exponentially from there. Now, that period of uncertainty and anxiety seems like a tiny blip. At the time, it felt like the end of everything.

The best way to get through those first few months is to remember that every moment you spend with your baby is an investment. The more time you spend with him or her, the more you deposit into your relationship account; the more familiar you become to your baby, the more comfortable you feel with your baby, the more confident you feel as a father. All that just by spending time. For me, it helped to incorporate Special Daddy Time into every day. So, set up a time, and make sure everyone in your family knows about it so no one will intrude. It's up to you what you do with your Special Daddy Time, but here are a few ideas.

**Hold her.** You don't have to do anything. Just hold her, bare chest to bare chest. Newborns—especially premature babies—really benefit from being close to you and your warmth. Sit anywhere you're comfortable and just lay her on your chest or hold her so her chest touches your chest. Put a blanket over her so she stays warm. To make it even more special, read to her. It doesn't really matter what you read or say, as long as she hears the sound of your voice and feels your warmth. She may even fall asleep. In fact, you may fall asleep, too.

**Feed him.** If your partner is breastfeeding, ask her to pump a little bit every day so you can give your baby a bottle. Your baby needs to know that you, too, can take care of her hunger needs.

**Take a walk with her.** You can use a baby carrier or a stroller.

**Read, talk, or sing to him.** She just needs to hear the sound of your voice, so anything you read is most likely fine: *Sports Illustrated*, an Abraham Lincoln biography, etc. (Maybe don't read her your work papers, though—you don't want her to feel your stress!)

**Hold your partner while she holds your baby**. This is another good way to build intimacy and closeness in your family.

**Change or dress her**. Again, she needs to know you can meet her needs. Not only does changing her diaper or her clothes help you to build a relationship with her, it's also one-on-one time that you'll find yourself cherishing— and you'll ease the burden on your partner.

**Trim his nails**. Babies' fingernails and toenails grow fast and can cause quite a bit of damage to your baby and you. You'll be doing everyone a favor. You could even just file them down a bit so they won't be so sharp.

Doing these things helped me spend more quality time with my children, but I wasn't sure if it was building a connection until Dorit and Lucas smiled at me. I believe the first months are the hardest for men because in their first few months, babies don't do anything but need a lot. We end up giving a lot without receiving anything visible in return, some reward for our efforts, like a smile or a hug or playtime. They sleep, they eat, they poop, and then they sleep some more—not always in that order. But when my children started to smile and react a little, I was able to relate to them more. And this was when we truly began forging our strong bond.

Soon, when it was time for my little girl to be put into her crib, she would reach out for me, and when I would tell Lucas to have a good night's sleep and that Daddy loved him, his crying would often subside. I had thought it would be like this right from the beginning. I hadn't realized that I would have to work so hard to build the connection. But it was worth it.

## Blazing a New Parental Trail

I've spent much of my life trying to unlearn what my parents taught me, and it has left me feeling a void within. It's very hard to *not* be something. Following a path is much easier than creating your own, but creating one is just what Gem and I have found ourselves trying to do. We have a pretty good idea of the kind of people we hope our children will be, but it's in the details where everything gets fuzzy and scary.

When my children were very young, I found myself looking externally for help in blazing a new parental trail. Most people learn much of what they know about parenting from their own parents. For those of us with parents who didn't do such a good job, or who weren't around, there are no role models, no blueprints we want to follow, no way to know if we're doing okay or not. This was why I turned to external sources.

I'd always hoped there was a parenting handbook that would be given to me upon the birth of my children. Alas, when my twins were born, the only books I received had lots of pictures, and pages that didn't rip (though they can still be chewed, I learned). I thought that without a blueprint, without a trail to follow, there would be no way to tell if I was doing a good job or not. "What if I'm screwing up and don't even realize it?" I joke about starting a therapy fund, but sometimes I do wonder if I should worry less about funding their college education and start monthly transfers to a therapy account.

Every night after I put our children to bed, I walked down the stairs and wondered if Gem and I were doing a good job. I was pretty sure my wife was, but I wasn't so sure about myself. Having unhealthy parents had left me no one to turn to for parenting advice. I couldn't ask my dad what he did when my sister and I wouldn't sleep through the night—he most likely wasn't there or would have no memory of addressing this situation. I couldn't ask my mother because she doesn't talk to me, hasn't for more than twenty years. Being isolated from my parents made me feel isolated as a parent, as if I were in it all by myself. This feeling of isolation also made it hard to really feel sure I was doing a good job. And raising two children at exactly the same time only made matters more complicated.

"Am I giving more to one than the other?" Sure, having twins might bring double the joy, but it also doubled my questions and feelings of doubt.

These doubts continued, and compounded significantly, up until about the time my children started learning how to talk. When they first started sitting up, I began to feel this very powerful connection with each of them. As they started moving around and reacting to the things that I did, the connection only grew stronger. But when they started to talk, I realized so much about the kind of father I was and wanted to be.

Turns out, the answers were always inside me.

"Daaaaaaaaddddddeeeeeeeeeeeeeeeee."

What I never realized in my search for answers outside myself was the power of that word, the power of being called "Daddy" by little beings who came to mean the absolute world to me. When they called out for me in pain because they got hurt, I didn't need a handbook to tell me to run to them. When they called out "Daddy" in the morning, I didn't need a parenting class to tell me they were ready for me to take them downstairs to start our morning rituals. When I came home from work and they ran to the door saying "Daddy's home," I didn't need good role models to tell me to relish the moment and hold on to the hug for as long as they let me. I never understood that so much of being a father is based on who I am and the love I feel for my children.

After being a parent to twins for almost four years (which must equal, like, eight years of parenting one child, right?), I realized three major things that helped me deal with blazing my own path.

1.  My goal should not be to give them the childhood I never had. I must provide for them what they need. I must end the cycle of difficult childhoods, the negative momentum my parents couldn't stop, and push all future generations of Schneiders in a positive direction. I won't be perfect, can't be perfect. But I can give my children the gift of unconditional love, support, and affection. In any family history that would be a gigantic step forward.

2. Awareness of what I went through is absolutely vital. I need to know what my parents did, what their parents did, and what their parents before them did. I need to know what I learned and absorbed from them about being a parent and relating to my children. This is the only way I can effect any change. I'm sure all parents have said something to their children and felt themselves channeling their parents. Imagine how many times we channel them but aren't aware of it. Awareness helps keep me from channeling the negative and dysfunctional patterns I experienced.

3. Continual personal growth helps me to be the person I want to be. I have worked very hard to develop new skills, new ways of communicating—to challenge myself to overcome the things with which I'm uncomfortable. I hope that with every single step I take, every personal challenge I overcome, my children will have it that much easier than I did, will have the head start they deserve.

For those of us blazing new trails as parents—paths that are very different from those our parents followed—without any handbooks or parenting classes to guide us, parenting is a very challenging experience. The trail is riddled with thorn bushes, sharp rocks, and large boulders. We can't repair a family that's been troubled for generations in one fell swoop, but we can begin that process with our children. I've come to believe that the best way to begin that process is to focus first on giving unconditional love to our children, while also being aware of what we went through and continuing to grow, continuing to become healthier physically, emotionally, and mentally. If I keep doing this, I know my children won't need to look externally for guidance on how to be a good parent, as I did; my wife and I will be good role models to help guide them.

## Practice, Practice, Practice

I've always disliked the "bumbling father" stereotype; it often makes fathers feel as though what they're doing isn't as important as what mothers do. If I thought my actions weren't as important as my wife's, then I wouldn't try as hard, wouldn't make as much of an effort, or be present as much as I could for my children.

When I was growing up, I never saw a man caring for his children the way I wanted to. I never saw a man changing diapers or feeding his baby. I had no idea how to do anything when it came to taking care of my babies when they were born. I just knew I wanted to.

Quite a bit of research shows that men will be involved as fathers if they

1. feel the paternal role is important
2. feel that being a father is a major part of their identity, and
3. feel confident and competent as parents.

Right off the bat, I knew being a dad was important to me. I didn't understand until later on how much being a father would become part of my identity, but it certainly did; I'm not only a father by any stretch, but it's one of the most important things I am and do, and I feel such pride in being a good daddy to my kids. It's certainly more important to me than how I perform in my job, for instance. My problem in the beginning, however, was that I was absolutely not confident and not comfortable as a parent.

My wife and I took parenting classes (specifically for parents of twins), but they were really focused on the process of becoming a parent versus actually being parents. Somehow my wife seemed to know how to be a mother, but being a father didn't come naturally to me. Sadly, I thought that was a sign there was something wrong with me, that maybe I wasn't fit to be a dad, that I would be a "bumbling dad" forever.

But studies have shown that once fathers understand they really do have a tremendous impact on their children's health and happiness, they become more involved—probably because they feel what they're doing makes a difference.

Not being able to feed my children because my wife was breastfeeding, not being able to put them to sleep because they had fallen asleep while nursing: these things made me feel as if I didn't have much to contribute. When Gem was nursing one child, I would hold the other, who was often screaming, wanting to nurse as well. Hiding in the bedroom of our two-room apartment with the door closed, trying to keep a screaming baby as quiet as possible so my wife could nurse our other child to sleep in the next room, didn't exactly build my confidence.

We all want to feel important. For men, that feeling can often be easier to achieve in the workplace than in the home, and I certainly felt that way. I knew how to do my job at the office, but at home, I was confused, unsure, and really nervous I was going to screw up. In my job, if I made a mistake, no one got hurt. But as a dad, it felt as though everything I did or failed to do could hurt my children—or even worse.

In the end, three things really made a difference for me during this period.

First, Gem was incredibly supportive of my being involved in our children's lives, and she stepped back so I could step in more. If she hadn't been so willing to share our parental responsibilities, I would have had to fight to build a connection with my children. That seems like a recipe for trouble.

Second, I realized I just needed some practice. I'd never factored in how little I knew about being a parent or an involved dad. The specifics were a lot harder than I ever imagined, but as with everything else, when you do something over and over again, you get better at it. Before I knew it, I was feeling more confident as a dad, which also gave me confidence to try new things, to take chances, to step outside myself and entertain, play with, and love my babies in new and different ways.

Third, it took time to get to know my kids. As I got to know them, I learned what this cry meant and what that face meant, what they looked like when they were tired or upset or hungry. And they got to know me, too. They learned that I was sticking around, and that I'd be there when they needed me, like their Mom, and that was good for all of us.

I don't believe it's a coincidence that as my confidence as a dad grew, so did my relationship with my children. I just needed to remember I was important to them, even if I didn't quite yet feel that way myself.

**Seven Pieces of Advice for a New Father**

A colleague of mine announced the birth of his baby girl, and then asked me if I had any advice for him. There was so much I wanted to say yet so little I thought I could really explain. In the end, I don't think I said anything at all. If only we could've performed a mind meld.

After I had some time to think about it, I did come up with a few things.

1. **Sleep when she sleeps**. It's a simple rule of thumb: "Is she sleeping? Then I should, too." I remember waking up to the sound of one of our children crying and seeing that the clock said 3:00. For a moment I didn't know whether it was early morning or afternoon—and then realized it didn't matter.

2. **Forget about cleaning up**. Having a clean house should now be considered a luxury. We recently visited friends who have two children under four. While I was impressed that the house looked so clean, our friends apologized for it being dirty. I realized that it looked clean to me because there was nothing on the floor to trip on and many free places to sit. Your baby won't care whether the house is clean or not, and any family or friends who visit will understand—especially if they have children themselves.

3. **Throw out expectations**. I had been working out at least three times a week for over a year before our kids were born. It took me eighteen months before I was able to start again—and I punished myself every day for failing to work out. But it was terribly unrealistic to expect it. I'd thought I would be able to do all the same things I'd done before our children were born, but there was an adjustment period. This is a completely new situation that no one can prepare you for, and it's best to focus first on caring for your family.

4. **Play a supportive role**. Before my children were born, I had only held a baby once or twice in my life and had never changed a diaper. But I understood that my primary role was to support my wife, especially because she was breastfeeding. Most new

mothers become so intently focused on taking care of their new baby and meeting her every need that they unintentionally neglect themselves. But to meet the nutritional and emotional needs of a baby, mothers need energy and rest. I made sure Gem ate and drank, and that she got as much rest as she could. By supporting her, I aided in the bond she was building with them, strengthened my bond with her, and also took steps to building my own bond with my children. And honestly, it also gave me a chance to learn from her.

5. **Reprioritize**. I wanted to be a great father. I also wanted to do well at work, lose weight and take care of my physical health, make sure I was okay psychologically, and be a good husband. There was no way I could do it all, though I tried. Part of the new-father process involves reprioritizing so that you can focus your limited energy and time on what you need to do to take care of your family and yourself.

6. **Practice, practice, practice**. One of the reasons I can do so much more now than in the beginning is that I now know so much more now about being a daddy and managing my new life. If you're like most new fathers, you probably don't know much about taking care of a baby. But soon, I promise you, it won't take thirty minutes to change a diaper or to get a bottle ready. With repetition comes a sense of ease in handling many of the daily tasks involved with raising a baby. As I got more and more accomplished at these daily tasks, I found I had a little extra energy because I didn't have to concentrate so much on each and every task (and I wasn't worried that I was going to screw it up).

7. **Take time to build the connection**. Mothers have an advantage when it comes to connecting with a new baby because they carried the child for nine months (in most cases). This connection can be very strong. Fathers often don't feel that same connection immediately (this was certainly my experience). This can be very disturbing to fathers—especially if they expected to immediately

feel a close bond with their child. But it doesn't mean there's anything wrong with you or that it doesn't matter what you do. You will build your relationship with your child just as you build any other relationship. By being there for her, talking to her, holding her, and taking care of her, you'll soon find the connection between the two of you growing. By the time she starts to speak, you'll likely marvel that you once didn't feel strongly connected to her.

This certainly isn't everything you need to know about being a father, but if I'd heard just a few of these pieces of advice when my kids were born, those first few months would've been a lot easier. Hopefully, these tips can help free you to be the best father you're capable of being. If you had told me I would feel as comfortable and confident as a father as I do now when I first started, I most likely wouldn't have believed you. Now, I understand I will only continue to grow as a father, and as a man.

## Juggling Life as a New Father

After my twins were born, I was constantly withdrawing from my time and energy accounts, but they were already overdrawn. It became impossible to juggle all of the priorities in my life, and some things fell by the wayside. It took more than twelve months before I felt as though I could just keep up with all of the changes in my life.

The biggest challenge was that there were still the same number of hours in the day but I had so much more to do. In order to keep my job and earn money to support my family—especially since my wife was home taking care of our children—I had to work just as hard, but on less sleep. At the same time, to be a good father and build a connection with my children, I needed to be home as much as possible. And so, I had to complete the same amount of work, with the same level of accuracy, in less time, so I could go home earlier.

Of course, being home was far from a break. I had so much to learn as a father, and it was physically, emotionally, and mentally exhausting. (And don't forget the lack of sleep.) I no longer had down time at home anymore, and I certainly didn't have the same level of energy and focus as I did before my children were born. Many things I used to do without much effort were now too difficult. Working out? I tried. I can't tell you how many times I thought about it, and I even set the alarm clock to get up early a few times, but I just couldn't do it. I would press snooze until it was time to get ready for work all the while cursing myself for not getting up. Hobbies? Hanging out with friends? I was too busy learning how to change diapers, soothe screaming children, and exist on little to no sleep. It seemed as if I had lost the higher-functioning capabilities of my brain. I was a worn-out wind-up toy: just point me in the right direction and if there's anything left, I'll move forward. No creativity. No brainstorming. No insight. No ideas. I was working so hard at just surviving, at just getting through each day, that I had nothing left with which to experience life, to actually live it. Those months are such a blur.

It wasn't just the big things (e.g., working out) that I wasn't able to do. Even smaller things that didn't involve much time were difficult. I was late paying bills, which I'd always been very good about. It was tough to keep in touch with friends and family, which made me feel isolated and alone. I felt I had no control at all (and I'm a man who has been called a control freak more than once). I couldn't exercise, but I couldn't stop eating things like chocolate, either. At the office, anyone who needed a chocolate fix knew where to go: my desk, which had a chocolate drawer. I didn't like who I was becoming.

To make matters worse, the lack of working out and the incredible increase in my chocolate consumption caused me to gain what I refer to as the "Twin Twenty." My clothes stopped fitting comfortably, and I absolutely did not like the way I looked in the mirror. But I couldn't seem to do anything to stop it from happening. I couldn't keep up with my life. I was too busy beating myself up to understand what was going on.

Fortunately, when our twins started to sleep better at night, around eleven months, I began to regain some of my higher-level brain functions. I was able to think about more than just getting through the day. A little more sleep really does make a difference. I was also becoming better at being a daddy. Things that I once really had to concentrate on, such as changing their diapers, feeding them, and getting them dressed, I could now do (almost literally) in my sleep. This freed up some energy for other things. I still wasn't able to work out, but I was getting better about handling our finances again; it helped that I now had a better idea of what day it was. Frustratingly, I still had difficulty exercising any willpower.

Most important, this clearing of my mind allowed me to start understanding what had been happening to me. I was completely maxed out, trying to be a good employee while working fewer hours and trying to be a good husband and daddy in the few hours I had with my family; I had nothing left for anything else—including me. I had too many high-level priorities and the least amount of time and energy I'd ever had. Things had to give, and they did.

Finally, at around sixteen months, I felt as if I'd walked out of a long, dark tunnel. Thankfully, the light at the end wasn't an oncoming train, but life. For fifteen months I'd spent almost every single ounce of energy I had on pure survival. Now, I could live life once again. Because work and being a father and husband were taking a little less energy, exercise moved up on my priority list, and sleep moved down a notch.

I had survived. And I even began to feel as though I could start building up a little reserve in my time and energy accounts for whatever would come next. I knew I would need it.

**I Am Their Daddy; Their Daddy Is I**

One of the most important things I've learned from being a father is that who I am as a person doesn't matter nearly as much as the fact that I am my children's father. Having a child (or twins) means stepping into an incredibly unique role, separate from oneself. Men who understand that the role of father is bigger than themselves end up having stronger, healthier relationships with their children.

In the beginning, I felt extremely inadequate. I didn't feel comfortable as a father and thus struggled to be the kind of father I wanted to be. I have come to learn that many dads feel the same way, and that their lack of confidence in the role is made worse if they're the primary breadwinners. Their jobs take them away from the house, giving them less time to practice being fathers. Soon, they begin to believe that since their children are getting along just fine without them, they aren't needed—they have nothing to contribute.

"What can I give them that their mother can't give?" some dads think. "Why would what I say really matter to them?"

I used to think this way. In fact, I did for a long time. However, I've been able to shift my perspective. I can see that what my children's father does is important to them. That's the key.

I am their daddy. Their daddy is I.

Whether or not I feel as though my attention, my love, my time has real value or worth, the fact that I am their daddy makes all that I do and say extremely important to my children. You know what? It's awfully scary, the power of parenting. But it has helped me do things I never thought I could do. It has helped me be more than myself. In the end, it isn't about me—it's about my children and trying to help them be as healthy and happy as humanly possible.

I've been able to shift my perspective for a couple of reasons. The first is that I think about what I wanted, but never got, when I was growing up. When I'm not sure what to do, I think about what little Jeremy needed in a similar situation all those years ago and try to be that kind of dad for them. The second is I began thinking about being a dad as a role to play when I wasn't sure what to do. If I was playing a good dad on TV, what would that character do in this situation? Then I tried it.

Understanding my role as a father, as Daddy to my children, has given me the freedom to stretch beyond the confines of my personality, beyond my upbringing, beyond myself, to better be what my children need me to be. This in turn has made me feel more comfortable with not only being a father, but also with myself. I've become the role, the Daddy, and no longer feel I'm pretending to play it.

**Seeing Myself through My Children's Eyes**

Most of us don't think of ourselves as heroes, or role models, or the ultimate male or female, or essential to anyone. But our young children see us that way. In my kids' minds, I am required, essential to their existence, whether I feel that way or not. Everything I do is seen from the eyes of children utterly dependent on me. It's a power that is difficult and frightening to comprehend. I never imagined I could be this important or have this much impact on another person.

Gem and I are careful about the language we use in front of our children because toddlers drink in language like a dehydrated camel. We've had that terrible experience of hearing them repeat a curse word we said. In fact, they spent two days periodically reminding us of that special word. Children absorb behaviors this way too, though many of us don't give our actions the same consideration we do our language.

My children don't know I make mistakes every day. They don't know that there's so much I feel unsure about as a father. They see me through the same lens I viewed my own parents through. I remember being a little boy and hearing my father slide his feet on the steps to our front door. To me, that sound was, and still is, the sound of being an adult, a man. Whenever I wore nice shoes, I would try to create that same sound, walking up those same steps. The sound was never quite the same, but it was close enough to make me feel, for a brief moment, as if I had achieved something.

I wonder what things are defining what it means to be an adult or a man for my children—probably more than I'll ever be aware of, but I do know that my water bottle is significant. I try to drink a lot of water, and my kids always want to drink from my bottle. When I take a big drink, at least one of my children almost always takes a big gulp from a sippy cup at the same time. Maybe when they're a bit older, drinking from their own water bottles, holding them at a certain angle, when the air in the bottle makes a certain noise, they'll feel as if they've achieved the same sense of momentary adulthood I did when I slid my feet up the steps to my front door.

So much of my children's lives are spent trying to be or show that they're more grown up than they really are. Whether they're figuring out how to turn the lights on or off, wearing our shoes, or getting in and out of their booster seats themselves, they struggle daily to be like Gem and me. I don't usually find people who want to be like me, but at home are these two adorable little beings striving to do what I do, be the way I am, every day.

They are watching, observing, learning. And this makes everything I do important, gives meaning to even the most meaningless tasks. It makes my mistakes feel huge, as if I need to contribute extra to their therapy fund, while positive things seem fleeting and temporary. Listening to music together helps them appreciate it more, and feel more comfortable building their own connection to songs and artists. Reading books with them helps them enjoy reading because they enjoy the time we spend together reading. Being affectionate shows them that it's okay to show how we feel. Arguing with my wife shows them how we try to solve our problems. Eating dinner together without the TV on sends a message about the importance of family dinner. Taking my vitamins shows them the importance of taking care of oneself.

Everything I do sends a message, and that makes me a bit paranoid. I know I will make mistakes, that there are things I won't do well every single time, but it's very hard to maintain the awareness that I am everything to my children, that I am the model for being human, when I struggle with being human myself each and every day. But I do know that trying to heighten my awareness of this issue challenges me to be a better father, a better person—for them, if not for myself.

I'm pretty aware of my issues, and knowing that my children absorb everything I do, I'm working extra hard to overcome these issues—especially around my children. My self-image has never been all that good; I've never seen myself as a good-looking guy and have often made jokes about that. When I started making those jokes in front of my children, I suddenly realized the message I was sending and didn't like it. I think my children are beautiful, and I want them to think that about themselves. It's not enough that I tell them every day how beautiful or intelligent they are if they see me putting myself down or not valuing myself. I need to remind them how wonderful they are, but I also need to think the same way about myself. Again, for them, if not for me. They deserve the best, and I've finally realized that I do, too.

I don't believe for one second we can or should be perfect—in fact, that would send a terrible message to our children. But I do believe that if my children see me working on my own issues, trying to be healthier, they will learn it's okay to not be perfect. They will learn that facing our problems is the best way to deal with them, to grow, to become who we want to be, and that, in the end, the process lasts a lifetime.

If that's the kind of role model I am for my children, I will be quite happy about that.

# Chapter Two

# Building Your Bond

*One of the best things I've learned since becoming a father is that almost everything is a bonding opportunity. I had thought that bonding required something specific, required me to be a certain way with my children, but every single moment with them is a chance to build a closer and deeper relationship. The trick is to find the things that click for you and your child. Don't do what you (or others) think should be done, but whatever works based on your child's reactions.*

## Doing Nothing Is Just As Special

One Friday night, Gem and I had friends over for Shabbat dinner (a special Friday night dinner celebrating the Jewish Sabbath; this was our friends' first Shabbat).

The dinner was lovely. That was the good part.

The bad part was that we didn't even start to get our toddlers ready for bed until way past their bedtime, and then Lucas started feeling sick to his stomach and kept having to go to the bathroom. I finally walked out of their room around ten o'clock that night (one and a half hours later than normal). He woke up around two with a stomachache and I finally got him back to sleep around three. I had trouble getting back to sleep, now feeling sick to my stomach as well, but finally drifted off around four. He was up again at five. Again I got him back to sleep, and then he woke up for good at 7:45 a.m. I was exhausted and felt terrible.

Unfortunately, Gem had a consulting gig for a few hours that morning and had to leave. I really wasn't sure how I was going to get through it, but it turned out to be very nice.

That morning with my children made me realize that I'd never had time alone with them. I would come home from work to the chaos of the evening rush, and on the weekends we usually did something as a family. I'd never had the chance to just hang out with my children at home, just the three of us.

For a while that Saturday I felt so sick that I could only lie on the couch. Thankfully, it was raining so hard that one of our neighbors was building a boat in his front yard, so I didn't have to worry about going out. My children took turns cuddling with me. Cuddling with my children—what a luxury.

We started watching *Mulan*—I'd never watched a movie with them before—and Dorit had a great idea: "You know what would be fun? We should have popcorn. You know, popcorn with movie?" And it was delicious, both the popcorn and the experience. Normally, the three of us would go to the zoo or the beach or the mall or shopping. We'd "do" something. This was nothing. I barely moved off the couch all morning. We just basked in the relaxing time together. I realized what I was missing out on going to work every day and not being around.

That morning helped me understand that to have special time with my children, I didn't have to DO something. Being together could be special as long as we enjoyed each other.

Mental note: this is a good thing to remember.

## Positive Ripple Effects

For a couple of years now, I've been writing articles that focus on helping dads develop better relationships with their children, and I always suggest that every day they ask their kids this question: "What did you do today while Daddy wasn't around?" I tried to ask my children this every day not only because I wanted to hear their answers, but also because I thought there was something so special for them in the telling. It showed them that what they did was important to me—even if I wasn't around when it happened.

I had a pretty good idea of some of the "little" things I needed to do to help my children grow up with a sense of confidence and high self-esteem, to grow up feeling loved by me. What I didn't understand was the ripple effect of these little actions. I was so focused on trying to be there for my children, on making sure they knew they were loved without a shadow of a doubt, that I often forgot to think about what my actions were teaching them.

One night we were having dinner at our favorite local dining establishment, Gino's. I took Dorit to the bathroom, and just as I placed her on the toilet, I asked her what she'd done that day.

"We goed to the playground."

"You went to the playground?"

"We went to the playground."

"Did you go on the slide?"

"No."

"Did you climb?"

"No."

"You went to the playground and you didn't slide and you didn't climb?"

"We swinged!"

"You swung on the swings?"

"Yeah, we swung on the swings. Daddy?"

"Yes?"

"Tell me about YOUR day!"

"Okay," I said, a big smile on my face. "I took the train to work. I missed you. I worked. I missed you. I had lunch with some friends. I missed you some more. I took—"

"What kinds of friends?"

"Good friends."

"Oh, I thought they were bad friends."

I grinned. "I try not to have any bad friends."

"Oh … What … What was … what names of …"

"What are the names of my friends?"

"Yeah."

"One is named Margaret."

"Margaret."

"The other is named Wilamena."

"Wilamena … That tickles my tongue." She giggled.

I giggled too. "It tickles your tongue?"

"Yeah. What else, Daddy?"

"Well, let's see. After lunch I worked some more and—"

"I know! You wrote a website called *Two Okapis* about Lucas and me."

"Actually, I wrote about you guys on the train in the morning."

"Really?"

"Oh yeah."

(It might not excite her as much when she realizes that I write about the conversations we have while she's sitting on the toilet.)

This was when my kids began asking me about my day because they wanted to know what I did when I wasn't around them. I often forgot how important I was to them, and when I would see it (through the way they asked about my day or about my friends), the feeling was pretty wonderful. They wanted to know because I matter to them, just like they matter to me.

All the different things I did to show them I loved them, they mirrored with their own unique style, showing me that they loved me too.

I'd never imagined an okapi lovefest could feel so good.

## Los Tres Amigos Thursdays

After spending over three years focusing on our children's physical and mental health, Gem started taking a yoga class on Thursday nights. We were both happy that she was finally taking the time and had found the peace of mind to do something for herself (relatively) guilt-free. Of course, while it may have been almost guilt-free (is anything we as parents do for ourselves completely guilt-free?), it was not trouble-free.

The problem was that to go to yoga, she had to leave in the middle of dinner. As you can imagine, this was not the best timing. We quickly decided to "market" these nights to the kids as a chance for some "daddy time"—Los Tres Amigos (the three friends) time. While Dorit was totally down with that (as Gem said, "She LOVES her Daddy"), Lucas was not so keen on losing Mommy. Before she left that first Thursday, he cried throughout dinner, saying, "Mommy, I really, really, really, really, really don't want you to go." The boy knows how to get his point across—I had to give him that. When she did finally leave, he was a wreck. Despite my displeasure at his getting so upset, I held him while he cried, and then Dorit joined in and very soon he felt better. We listened to music and had a wonderful time. Until I took them to bed. Then they turned into spawns of the devil and made the going-to-sleep process utterly and completely miserable, making me question everything I did as a father.

The next week, unwilling to go through that again, I suggested Gem leave early so we wouldn't have to go through the dinner of tears and "really, reallys." But then we decided that instead of her leaving early, I would take them out for dinner. Lucas cried some more, but as soon as the car started moving he got very excited about going to Friendly's as Los Tres Amigos. The kids talked about how much they missed Mommy but behaved much better.

The third week, I took them out for dinner again and Lucas didn't get upset at all—even though he knew Mommy was going to yoga. When we got back home, I put them to bed, and the experience was much nicer (we got to read new books from the library).

What really turned Gem's evenings away into something special was the fact that I had time alone with my kids. And when I saw it as special and made it special (by going out just the three of us, Los Tres Amigos), my children began to see it as special, too (which, of course, also made it easier for Gem to do something for herself without feeling too guilty). And before we knew it, Thursday nights became something we all looked forward to instead of dreaded.

## Making Note of How I Feel

One morning I had to leave for work before my children were awake. Since Lucas had really wanted to see me, I left him a note. On construction paper in several different colors, I told him how proud of him I was, what a great sleeper he was, and that I loved him. I even drew a stick figure with hair. (I am quite terrible at drawing. I even have trouble drawing decent stick figures. Seriously.)

Gem told me later that he absolutely loved it. LOVED it! He was so excited about it—especially the crude stick-figure drawing—because he thought it was him and something about my drawing him made him feel special. How many times had I done something special for him that didn't have any impact? It was pretty nice to have done something by accident that had special meaning for him.

I had also left him five chocolate chips. Gem and I had been trying to find a reward for him for sleeping through the night and using the potty, something that he would enjoy earning. For Dorit, mini M&M's were a big deal, but they didn't do much for Lucas. Then I remembered one of his "remember whens." My children would sometimes ask me if I remembered something that held meaning for them. For instance, Lucas had once asked me, "Remember when we had chocolate chips?" So, I theorized that chocolate chips were something he connected with me, so I left him chocolate chips. He loved them. That night he even stated that if he slept through the night he'd get chocolate chips. He got it!

He also told Gem he wanted another note, but she forgot to tell me. Thankfully, she wrote a little note to cover for me (she's an artist so she had to drop her skill level significantly), and Lucas loved it as well. That night at dinner, Lucas looked at me from across the table and asked if he could have another note in the morning. After he and his sister went to bed, I played around on the computer and created a note for Lucas that had a picture of the two of us; it told him how proud of him I was, what a good sleeper he was, and how much I loved him. Then I found a picture of Dorit and wrote her a note telling her how proud I was of her for doing so well with the potty. I also told her what a great sleeper she was, because she had always been an incredible sleeper and had gotten nothing for it except having to listen to Lucas scream. When I was congratulating Lucas once, she said, "I'm a good sleeper, too." It was true, and it was easy to take that for granted. I put his note on the breakfast table (with his five chocolate chips) and put her note on her potty (Gem's idea) with her five mini M&M's.

The notes became a regular thing, and the neurotic me worried that they would be the death of me—every night, I needed to come up with a new note for each of them, something that would make them feel good and express how I felt about them. However, the rest of me was amazed and proud. I had managed to find another way to connect to my children while I was away at work, another way to build our relationship, another way to make sure they always knew how strongly I felt about them.

Not too shabby for a few minutes of "work."

## Doing Something New

My little girl started doing something new one week, and I found myself really enjoying it. My children have always loved music, mostly because my wife and I really love music. I almost never do anything without it, and I firmly believe the iPod is one of the greatest inventions of all time. So, what did my little girl start doing?

Dancing.

At four-and-a-half years old, she wasn't exactly going to clubs and dancing the night away. But that was precisely why I was enjoying it so much: she had started on her own, she did it anywhere she wanted, and she often did it accompanied by only the music in her head (though sometimes the music in stores was inspiration as well).

She would start with finger snapping (she is an excellent snapper), and would then move her arms and eventually the rest of her body. Sometimes she would close her eyes and sometimes she would keep them open, watching me to see my reaction. My reaction was pretty much the same every time:

Joy. Pleasure. A big smile. I was a mirror of what she was feeling because watching her dance, I felt it, too.

I am a dancer—in my own way. I love to dance to music, letting myself be free, letting myself be who I really am, unchained from who I think I'm supposed to be or should be. And I hoped that my little dancing girl was reaching that same point in herself. She too seemed to be freeing herself, being her true self, letting her real self shine through. And every time she saw my positive reaction, I hoped she would know how happy I was to see her true self.

The problem was that I was slightly embarrassed when she did it publicly. I knew I shouldn't have been, and I knew she might even have been able to feel my embarrassment despite my other positive reactions. Finally I asked myself, "What's the best way to overcome this awkwardness?"

I began dancing with her.

We would often move around the living room, dancing to the music in her head or that she was snapping or humming for us. It was lovely to be so free with my little girl.

But the pinnacle of these experiences happened at a sandwich restaurant. My little girl needed to go to the bathroom. I took her and when she was finished, she realized she could hear the music much better in the bathroom. My first reaction when she started dancing was to ask her to stop, but I caught myself. I didn't want her to stop being herself, to hide herself—especially from me.

So I joined her.

Yup, my little girl and I danced our hearts out in the bathroom, snapping our fingers, moving our arms, swaying our hips to the music.

And when the song was over, I was so excited I wanted to run out into the restaurant and tell everyone what had just happened.

I settled for telling my wife, and that was pretty good.

## A Special Pre-Thanksgiving Moment

It was the day before Thanksgiving, and for the first time in many, many years, I wasn't guessing whether I'd be able to go home early. I knew I'd have to stay late to deal with an urgent issue—a depressing reality of my new position. Before I left that morning, I stepped into my children's room to say good morning and, unfortunately, goodbye.

"Good morning! Where's my hug?" My two gorgeous children (almost five years old) ran into my arms, almost knocking me off balance.

"You smell good, Daddy," said Lucas. "You smell like cologne."

"That's good because I'm wearing cologne."

"You smell like the cologne I like." He started to walk away, bummed.

"You know, tomorrow is Thanksgiving," I said. "If you want, we can both put on the cologne before we go to Abuelita's." His face lit up like the North Star.

*Clack, clack.*

"Hey," I asked my kids. "When you shake your butt, does it make a sound?" I shook my butt again.

*Clack, clack.*

Of course, they shook their butts—what almost-five-year-old is going to pass up that opportunity? But alas, no *clack.*

I did it one more time before turning around. They burst out laughing when they saw my iPod sticking out of my back pocket and the earbuds clacking together, making that sound.

I said goodbye and started to walk down the hallway, but turned back.

"Hey, you know what?" They turned their heads. "Do I have to go to work tomorrow?"

"NO!"

"Does Mommy?"

"NO!"

"How about Friday?"

"NO!"

"And Saturday?"

"NO!"

"And Sunday?"

"NO!"

"A four-day weekend! Four days together!"

"Yeah!"

We did a mini-dance for a few moments before I said goodbye again, telling them I loved them. As I was about to leave the house, my children started coming down the stairs.

"You want one more hug?" I asked my little boy, who looked a little sad to see me leaving. We hugged, and he kissed my arm and my hand, his way of expressing love and affection, a gesture I was honored to receive.

I then hugged my little girl and walked out the door thinking about what a perfect morning it had been, despite knowing I had to work late. I loved my children and my wife and they knew it, and they loved me and I knew it. What else could I ask for in this world?

Parenting can be so stressful, so overwhelming, so exhausting. But moments like these, special moments, perfect moments, bonding moments, always remind me just how wonderful life with my family is. Moments like these were what I was thinking about the next day when it came time to say what we were thankful for that year.

## On the Path to Becoming a Man

I've had the pleasure of experiencing one of the true joys of fatherhood: helping my son on his path toward manhood.

When I was a kid, my dad worked eighty to ninety hours a week and I rarely saw him; he was out of the house by six in the morning and often didn't come home until after I was in bed. I certainly never got to see him get dressed, shave, use cologne, shine his shoes, or anything like that—the little things that can help a little boy feel as if he's getting a glimpse of the path toward being a man.

The fact is, children define being a woman or a man based on what they see their parents do. The few times I was awake when my father came home from work, I would listen to the sound of his feet as he walked up the steps. He slid his feet on each step, and that sound still means adulthood to me. It's still a sound of being a man. But Lucas doesn't have to guess what things are associated with manhood the way I had to growing up. I can actually make these things explicit, and there is something incredibly empowering, if a little scary, about this. It's scary to think that what I do will define manhood for him, and it makes me wonder if I'm a good representative of what it is to be a man. Well, I may not be typical, but I think I'm the kind of man both Gem and I hope Lucas will become—that's the empowering part.

On New Year's Eve one year, the four of us were getting ready to go to a friend's house for a get-together. We were all dressing up, and Lucas looked absolutely dashing. (One of the great things about Gem is that she dressed our children so well when they were young, which I think made a big difference in helping them feel good about themselves and their own sense of style—I didn't know anything about fashion until she and I started dating.) He wanted to put sneakers on, though, and was very insistent about it. Gem tried to dissuade him to no avail, so she sent him to me (probably hoping I had learned something from all of the fashion tips she's given me over the years).

I, of course, told him that his dress shoes would be so much better. He didn't seem to agree. And then I had a thought.

"Wanna see the shoes I'm going to wear?"

He perked up. "Yeah!"

I pulled my beautiful black wing tips out of the closet. They desperately needed a shining. Another thought.

"Hey, Lucas. Want to help me shine them?"

"Yeah! What's shine?"

"Well, sometimes shoes need to be cleaned to make them look shinier."

"Oh."

I got my little shoe-shine tool and went to work.

"Can I do that, Daddy?"

"Of course."

And my son shined my shoes for me.

Putting aside the bonus of free labor, I remember thinking the moment was special, that he and I were bonding over something that he would think about in terms of being a man. He then put his nice shoes on without any complaint.

Then it was time for cologne. Lucas has quite an impressive sense of smell, and always notices how we all smell and whether he likes the scent or not.

"You want some cologne, Lucas?"

"Yeah. Which one do you smell like, Daddy?"

"I'm going to use this one," I told him, pointing to one of my three colognes.

"I want that one, too." The kid makes my heart explode with love.

"Okay, give me your hand." He gave me his wrist. "That's how Mommy does it. You know how we do it?" He shook his head. "Here, give me your hand." He gave it to me and I sprayed it. "Put it on your cheeks. Like this." I showed him how I do it.

"Then you know what I do?"

"What?"

I sprayed some on his hair and then my hair. I don't know why, but this has always been the way I do it, and it seemed like it would be fun for him.

As we walked out of the room, my arm around his little shoulders, I was struck by how incredible sharing these things with him had been. I had helped him begin that long journey toward being a man. I realized that the process itself, the journey, could bring us even closer together.

**Potty Time Is Bonus Bonding Time**

For many parents, "potty training" (a very poor term—we're not training dogs, we're teaching kids) is riddled with challenges. I didn't want to push our kids too hard or too fast because I thought they might fight us and refuse to even try. However, I also knew that if we didn't start soon enough, we would start getting pressure from daycares and preschools. And of course, we also had hopes of throwing out our Diaper Genies. So, we embarked on our potty-teaching journey, with a focus on trying to teach them something new, trying to help them become big kids. What I didn't realize was that this was another opportunity to strengthen my relationship with my children.

To be honest, the whole topic, even just saying "pooping" and "peeing," made me very uncomfortable. I struggled to talk about it, and for months I wouldn't let my children come with me to the bathroom. But because I had such issues with this process, I worked much harder to make my children feel comfortable, to avoid infecting them with my perspective.

It's ironic that when we're potty teaching our children, we're helping them become more independent but the process itself makes them temporarily more dependent on us. They need us to show them what to do, to tell them they're doing well, and to let them know it's okay when they have an accident. Their understanding of potty teaching is based solely on our reactions to what they do. This is where the opportunity to build an even stronger relationship with your child presents itself.

When my little girl first started using the potty, I didn't handle it all that well. She would sit on the toilet for twenty minutes, and in the mad rush of trying to get her and Lucas to bed at night, we never had that kind of time. But I couldn't tell her that! I tried to be calm, so she wouldn't feel forced to do something quickly.

Once I realized that these bathroom sessions took some time, I started taking books with me. She would "read" me a book she knew by heart, or we would look at a book of the alphabet, or name the animals in a nature book. It quickly became special time for Daddy and Dorit. And then, whenever she asked me to come to the bathroom with her, I felt honored, special, that this time seemed to be as important to her as it had become to me.

One evening in particular demonstrated how important this process of potty teaching was, and how it can positively affect our relationships with our children.

We were at a little pizza place near our house with some friends when Dorit needed to go to the bathroom. In a stall, I sat her down on the toilet. She was still a bit too small for the public toilets, so I held her hands to help her keep her balance. She held on tightly, afraid of falling. When she said she was done, I lifted her off the toilet, back to safer ground, and she mumbled something.

"What, Sweetie Girl?"

"I love you, Daddy." My heart melted. It was as if she had said, "Thank you for being there for me, Daddy. Thank you for taking care of me, Daddy." It was one of the most heartfelt I love yous I'd ever heard from her.

Sometimes it's all about the destination, about achieving the goal. But when it came to educating our children about using the potty, the process itself was more special than I ever could have imagined. It could easily have been a very challenging time, but instead, it strengthened our bond.

## Surprising Obstacles

I'm not afraid of being affectionate with my children—of being close to them, holding them, playing with them. To my surprise, though, there was a time when two things made this harder to do, but I didn't know it until they were gone.

First were the safety rails on their beds. They prevented my children from falling, but they also prevented me from easily getting into bed for snuggles with them.

When Gem and I were in the process of selling our home, we removed the safety rails each day to make the kids' room look a little bigger for open houses. It really did open up the space. One night, we forgot to put the safety rails back on. Fortunately, nothing happened. No one fell out of bed. No one complained. No one missed them. So we didn't bring them back.

In the morning, I was able to easily sit on the edges of their beds to say hello. And when it was clear they weren't ready to get out of bed yet, I was able to climb in and cuddle with them or tickle them.

They really loved the physical closeness, and I really loved it, too. It became a major factor in our great weekends. When you start the day cuddling and tickling and playing together, you're off to a pretty good start.

Interestingly, the other thing that helped me get closer was getting rid of my glasses. I'd worn glasses my entire life, but I knew Lucas felt uncomfortable; in our family, he was the only one who didn't wear them. I thought that if I got contact lenses, he wouldn't feel so left out. What I hadn't realized was that wearing glasses had prevented me from lying down or roughhousing with my kids because I was always worried they would get broken. But once I got contacts, I could easily play with my kids without any worry about something bending or breaking.

Ditching the safety rails and glasses freed me up to be more playful, more fun, more loving with my children.

Who knew such seemingly small things could make such a big difference?

## The Joy of Watching Them Read

One of my favorite things as a parent has been seeing the leaps and bounds my children make in mental ability and agility. When they first began to speak, watching them struggle to form sentences and then succeed was such a joy. I knew I was watching their brains grow right in front of my eyes. I was watching a miracle. Speaking is something we take for granted, but for a child it's an accomplishment, a feat of unprecedented achievement. I've loved being a part of their growth, watching and helping, if possible, as they take each developmental step. When they began to learn to read, it was like the excitement I feel seeing my favorite artist live in concert.

I don't remember learning to read, so I don't remember what it felt like. But watching my children do so was one truly incredible experience. Somehow I'd been under the impression that something would snap in their brains and they would go from not reading to reading. Oh, silly me! It's a significantly more complicated process than that.

Lucas and Dorit had been able to write their names for some time, and they certainly enjoyed asking Gem and me to tell them how to spell things so they could write them down. "How do you spell 'Dear,' Daddy?" But then they started trying to sound out some words, and it became clear that they were ready to read. The seismic shift in our world happened while we were stuck at the optician's, waiting for Dorit's glasses.

Fumbling to find something to do to keep their interest, I led them to a candy machine. It was depressingly empty, but still had the names of the candies on the glass.

"Rrrr … uhhh … nnnnn … ttttt … sssss," Lucas said out of the blue.

"Try it a little faster," I said, quite excited.

"Rrrrunntttsss … Runts!"

"Yeah! Great job, Lucas." Of course, he had no idea what Runts were. After I told him, I looked around for more words he could try to read. I spotted a big advertisement with some easier words.

"Wwwww … aaaaaa … ttttt … What!" "Sssssss … eeeeeeeeeeee … eeeeeee … See!" On and on we went—I'd find words and he'd rise to the challenge. For me, parenting is made up of special moments, moments where something miraculous happens either in my relationship with my children or in their development, in their experience of the world, and I'm lucky enough to witness it. My little boy's realizing he could read these words was one of those amazing moments.

After leaving the optician's, I bought them a Backyardigans book specifically for beginner readers. As soon as I gave it to them, Lucas went upstairs to read by himself. I could just imagine my little boy lying on his bed reading his new book, still feeling a little shy about this new skill, not wanting to make his twin sister feel bad and not wanting to be distracted by his parents. Maybe he was only looking at the pictures, but maybe he was practicing his new talent.

That night, I read from the book for their bedtime story. At one point, Lucas started reading one of the sentences and I could barely control my excitement. The trick with Lucas is to find the balance between support and enthusiasm without overwhelming him—because he, like his dad, can be overcome with the intensity of other people's emotions. I think I got the balance okay that night because he kept trying for a little bit longer; long enough for me to know he was actually reading sentences.

After that day, if he was in the mood he would read signs along the road, on the TV, in books—he'd even read some stories on his own. Then Dorit went through a similar process. I had taken out some beginning-reader books from the library, and she began sounding out and reading words and even some sentences. I once again felt excitement, pride, and elation. It was incredible to be present for the process again.

Soon, Lucas went one step further by adding a little twist to our goodnight ritual.

"What are your happy thoughts, Lucas?"

"D-A-D-D-Y, M-O-M-M-Y, D-O-R-I-T, and L-U-C- A-S."

For the first time, I felt I truly understood the power of reading.

## Want a Tour, Daddy?

One time when my children were toddlers, I took a day off work to take them to day camp. Gem usually took them, but she needed to sleep that day because she'd picked up her parents at the airport at four in the morning. And I'm glad I took this time to do it.

Getting them ready was something like a nightmare, though. I'd never done it before, and not knowing how much time I needed made the morning much more stressful than it should've been. Plus, Lucas was overtired and challenged me on every single thing I asked him, which only added to my frustration.

But somehow we got out the door on time and enjoyed a leisurely walk to camp (only a couple of blocks away). When we got there, I met their teachers and saw the classroom (where they would attend preschool in the fall). My first thought was that it was small—but then, all of the children in the class were small, too.

As my children started to play with something, I said, "Can I have a hug?" They both gave me really good, tight hugs (I swear one of the teachers said "Awww"), and I told them I loved them and would pick them up when it was over. Then I walked out the door. Not a single sound. They didn't get upset or anything. I took that as a good sign.

Three hours later I was standing outside the classroom waiting with several mothers. When the teacher opened the door, Dorit started running toward me and got into trouble—apparently she was supposed to stay in her chair until she was called. But she didn't care. The teacher called her name while she was still standing, and then she ran the rest of the way to me. It was such a glorious feeling, knowing my little girl was so excited to see me.

"You want a tour, Daddy?"

"Absolutely!"

So she and Lucas gave me a tour of their classroom—a tour similar to the one they'd received when they came to my workplace. There was something special about seeing what they did, where they went, who they were with when they were at camp (which was exactly what they liked about coming to my office, I'm sure).

They showed me where they sat and painted, where they sang songs and listened to stories, where they played with the kitchens, the dolls, the food, the playhouses (which they really wanted), and all of the other things they did in that room.

Then we enjoyed a leisurely walk back home, just the three of us, holding hands, looking both ways before crossing the street ("No cars in sight!"), and examining any bugs or worms that happened to reveal themselves.

What else could a daddy ask for, frankly?

## Wrestling for Intimacy

"Ready? Get DADDY!" my five-year-old children would yell before they began their almost-coordinated attack on their target. Often, I'd be on the floor and they'd try to pin me down, to show they were stronger than I was.

But I knew the truth.

They didn't just want to pin me. They didn't just want to have fun. They also wanted to be physically close to me. They wanted another way of showing their daddy affection.

I'm not a macho guy. This may not come as a surprise to any of you who read my column regularly. While I've always been athletic and enjoy sports and competition, I'd never pictured myself as one of those dads who would wrestle with his children.

I'd always thought that this kind of physical activity was the "socially appropriate" way for a male to be affectionate with his children: "I'm not being touchy-feely: I'm being manly." But I'd also thought that this "manly" expression of affection often replaced real affection, and I'd never wanted to be like that. I've always been comfortable being affectionate with my children and am not afraid to show it. I'm touchy-feely and I'm cool with that.

But I reviewed some research on "wrestling," and it turns out children really benefit from this kind of physical closeness. It's not only good for their physical well-being, but it also provides an excellent way for parents (often fathers) to connect with their children both physically and emotionally. It also helps kids manage the highs and lows of emotion that occur during physical activity—particularly where competition is involved.

And it turned out that affection wasn't the only form of physical intimacy my children wanted and needed. I first noticed this with Lucas. We were playing around on the floor, and I'd tackled him to the ground to tickle him.

"Can you untrap me, please?"

I stopped and let him up, but then he came right back into the same position so I could tickle him some more. We kept this little routine going for several minutes. I'd tackle and tickle him, he'd ask to "be free," and then he'd come back.

At first glance, it seemed he didn't want to wrestle. And being trapped certainly wasn't high on his list of things to do before he got old. But then it became clear that he wanted me to be physical in that way with him. His enjoyment made it easier for me to get comfortable with this particular form of affection, and made the whole experience so much more fun.

Dorit also craved my affection. She was a daddy's girl, and it was wonderful. If a day or two went by and we didn't get enough time together, she would become very upset when I went to work. But even for her, the wrestling seemed very important. Hugs and kisses just weren't enough, didn't get her close enough to me. Wrestling, I think, made her feel more of a physical connection with me, more of a sense of intimacy.

They loved trying to "trap" me before I "trapped" them. If Lucas was "trapped," he would call out to Dorit to save him using her special super-powers, and vice versa. It was a game that became bigger than I ever expected, and more fun, too.

Maybe it was feeling my strength embracing them in a way that was different from a hug. Maybe it was the spontaneity of it. Maybe it was the combination of physical closeness and laughter. It's probably a combination of all these things that makes wrestling special.

If my children hadn't so freely and genuinely responded to wrestling, I probably would've missed out on another way of building intimacy with them. And I wouldn't have learned how much I enjoy being that close with them, too.

# Chapter Three

# It's 3:00 ... a.m. or p.m.?

*Crying woke me up. The clock read 3:00, and I didn't know whether it was a.m. or p.m. I realized it didn't matter; a baby was crying and needed food. Time was unimportant. Sleep was one of the more challenging issues I encountered as a parent, not only because I often didn't get enough, but also because as my children got older, nighttime was when their fears came out. It turned out that having a nightly ritual and becoming their Night Watchman made a huge difference in my relationship with them and in their ability to sleep through the night.*

## Night Watchman

When our twins finally came home from the hospital, four weeks after being born, Gem and I decided that she would get up with the kids at night because I had to go to work during the day. But this didn't work for very long for a number of reasons—mostly because I didn't like not being involved.

When we moved into our first house, ten months after they were born, and started trying to get them to sleep through the night, we decided that I would be the one to get up when our kids started fussing at night, instead.

I would become the Night Watchman.

I'm not sure I've ever loved a job more than this one. Yes, without a doubt, for years it was an exhausting job. And my day job suffered. But it changed my relationship with my children dramatically.

In the beginning, in the early days of my being a father, my kids didn't seem to like me. Oh sure, they loved Daddy, they were happy when I came home from work, but in every situation, they would rather have Mommy than Daddy. "Mommy do it," they would cry while I changed their diapers or read them books. "Mommy do it!" There aren't many worse words a father can hear his children scream.

But the truth was, their mother was not only a great mother—she was also with them all day long, meeting each and every one of their needs. They got used to her and how she loved and cared for them. And all the while I was at work. I was missing opportunity after opportunity, making them think I couldn't be there for them, though I desperately wanted to be.

How could I make the most out of the time I was home with them? Well, since there were only a couple of hours between when I came home and when we put them to bed, I would have to become the Night Watchman. We didn't call it that, of course, but that's what I was—and still am to this day.

I started putting them to bed—every single night—by myself. They fought it at first, because Gem and I used to put them to bed together, but they adjusted and got used to me. Soon it became a special time for me and my kids.

Then when they had trouble sleeping or cried out in the middle of the night, I was the one to go upstairs and take care of them, pick them up, soothe them, and show them they weren't alone, that they were loved.

It wasn't long before Gem and I would hear "Daddy" come through the monitor stationed on our bed in the middle of the night. The amazing thing was that I could hear them even without the monitor, and sometimes I was so attuned to them that I could feel, sense, when they were awake before they made a sound—even though they were upstairs and we slept downstairs. Being the Night Watchman gave me a connection to them that hadn't existed before.

But, more important was watching how they looked at, and treated, me differently. By my meeting some of their core needs, by being the parent that responded at night when they were scared or lonely, they learned that I could take care of them as well. And it changed everything. In fact, after I helped my boy start sleeping through the night after a particularly difficult couple of months, he began to look at me with such love, such awe, as though I had finally imprinted on his brain—I was his Daddy and nothing could ever change that.

I'd like to think my kids know I'll be there for them no matter what happens, just as they know their mother will be there for them. I also know that if they do, it's because of my job as the Night Watchman.

## Nightmares Waking Us Up

My little girl was having nightmares. This scared me because I have nightmares, too—have had them for as long as I can remember. Sometimes I'll go a couple of weeks without a good night's sleep. I worry that I've somehow given her the same problem.

The challenge was that she was only two years old. She had no understanding of the images in her head and no way to fully articulate what she was seeing or feeling. When I tried to talk to her about them, I felt as if I were speaking Swahili and she was speaking Chinese; we just couldn't understand each other.

One night I had a terrible nightmare and woke up very upset. Within two or three minutes, one floor above us, Dorit screamed and then started crying for Daddy. Gem wondered if my nightmare had triggered her nightmare. I wondered if the opposite might be true because when she woke up, I was already up and ready to be there for her. Or maybe I just wanted to believe that was true—I felt so guilty that she was having these nightmares, my nightmares.

For several nights she'd been crying out in her sleep, sometimes even saying "no." We would hear her thrashing around in her crib, moaning, but she'd somehow manage to quiet down on her own. Even when she was a baby, she would sometimes scream or cry out in her sleep, though thankfully, it almost never woke her up.

Sometimes when she woke up from her nap or in the morning, she was visibly upset. That was true this night as well; when I went into her room to pick her up, she was already standing up in her crib, and she latched on to me with all of her strength while still holding her woobie.

"Scared," she whispered as I lifted her out of the crib.

"Did you have a bad dream, Sweetie Girl?"

"Yeah, bad dream." She exhaled.

"Can you tell Daddy what it was about?"

"Yeah."

I waited a few seconds, but her head was leaning on my shoulder and she wasn't saying anything.

"What did you see, Dorit?"

"Regina."

"Oh."

Regina is the giraffe on *64 Zoo Lane*. It's not exactly a scary image, unless your child makes you watch it over and over and over again. Even as a toddler, my girl was incredibly verbal, and I was often blown away by the sentences she was able to put together. She and I had always had a special ability to communicate with each other. But trying to describe images in her brain that occurred only when she was sleeping and probably didn't make a lot of sense was just too much for my little girl.

I wasn't even sure if her dreams were scary in themselves or if she was scared by the fact that when she closed her eyes, all of a sudden there were images that she couldn't make go away. Maybe it was a little of both.

Another night, I could hear her gradually getting more and more upset. When she finally woke up, she cried out, "Sleep with Daddy? Sleep with Daddy?"

I went upstairs and picked her up. "Sleep with Daddy?" she repeated, louder and louder. We sat on the couch, her on my knee, her head resting against my shoulder.

"Sleep with Daddy?" she whispered.

"Are you okay, Little Girl?"

"Yeah."

I set her on the couch and grabbed some blankets from her bed. Then I picked her up and laid her down on the couch before lying down next to her, facing her, my arm on her back.

"Did you have a bad dream, Little Girl?"

"Yeah."

"Can you tell Daddy what you saw?" I asked gently. It was dark and our faces were only a few inches apart, our conversation only a whisper.

"Yeah."

"What did you see?"

"Elmo, Zoe."

I kissed her on the forehead and felt such immense love for this little girl. And I felt such helplessness. Had she really dreamed about Elmo and Zoe from *Sesame Street*? Yes, they are monsters, but not exactly scary ones. As I took off my glasses and put them out of reach, I reminded myself that I usually figured these things out. I just hoped I could figure out how to help her with this soon.

"Where are my glasses, Daddy? Where are my glasses?"

I laughed, a laugh of marvel and love. "They're downstairs, Sweetie Girl. You'll wear them again when you wake up in the morning."

"Right ... right."

I put my head on the pillow. She snapped her head up and said, "Go to sleep, Daddy. Go to sleep."

"Okay, Sweetie Girl. Let's go to sleep."

She put her head back down, and in a few minutes I heard the rhythmic sound of her breathing. Neither of us had any more nightmares that night.

In the morning, I reflected on the previous night. All this time I'd been feeling guilty, worrying that her nightmares had come from me. But I was missing something very important. I didn't need to help her understand her nightmares or dreams, or even explain what they were (how much would she have been able to understand, anyway?). I just needed to help her understand that the nightmares were mere aberrations, exceptions to the rule. I just needed to keep telling her and showing her that she was our special girl who was loved unconditionally. Being loved unconditionally was something I hadn't had as a child.

My childhood nightmares had been reflections of my real life: scary, confusing, and overwhelming, with no relief. My parents weren't there to wake me from my nightmares and banish them with love; my mother *was* my nightmare, and my father was simply not there for me. By helping my daughter feel safe and loved, I ensured her nightmares lost their power, their meaning. When she woke up from them, I was there, ready to give her a hug and a kiss and to remind her that she was my Sweetie Girl. This made the nightmares less scary for both of us.

## My Nightly Ritual

I always came home from work at the worst part of the day. After a ninety-minute door-to-door commute, I'd arrive home tired but knowing that the day was nowhere near over. Gem would be tired from having been with our twin toddlers all day by herself. And my children would also be tired from the day and ready to chill out, read some books, and go to sleep. The problem was that this was the most structured time of the day.

It started with dinner, which meant herding our kids into their chairs and trying to get them to eat. After a "relaxing" dinner, we had to nebulize them (for respiratory problems), change them, and brush their teeth before I took them upstairs to continue our nightly ritual.

There was always the danger that they would get so upset they wouldn't be able to go to sleep. We had recently gone through a stretch where they had difficulty going to sleep. It had been happening less frequently, but that worry was always there; I felt it every single night. And I felt it most acutely during the four transitions of our nightly ritual, because each transition brought them closer to going to sleep.

While I was turning on the lights, starting the music, and picking out books, they would often try to run around and jump on the sofa in their room—this was against the rules. "Bedtime. Time to wind down and get ready to go to sleep." This was the first transition, from being downstairs and having fun to being upstairs and preparing for sleep. I didn't want them getting all excited again, but almost every night they would start jumping on the couch and I'd have to tell them to stop. Starting the going-to-bed process with my yelling at them or threatening a time-out took the pleasure out of the experience right off the bat.

The best part of our nightly ritual would come next, though: reading our books. I usually picked books that I liked or that we had read together and I knew they really enjoyed. This way, I could read with enthusiasm and humor, which made it fun for all of us.

We'd snuggle together on the couch in their room, and for the most part they were attentive and focused. When we read a Dr. Seuss book, they liked trying to repeat some of the crazy sentences. If I messed up a line, we would all laugh. It was the only time in my life when I hoped I would make a mistake. But no matter how good this time was, I always worried about the next transition.

After we read our books on the couch, it was time to read one last book near their beds. Lucas was often fine with this transition, but this was when Dorit often started getting upset about their mother.

"But I miss Mommy," she would cry out, even though we'd just seen her ten minutes earlier. When this first started happening, I tried to talk to her about it. After that didn't work, I decided it was better to cut her off at the pass. I would interrupt her before she got too upset and try to distract her—because once she was upset there was no stopping her.

"I got mucous!" she'd cry out. Then she'd start sniffing, trying to prove how much mucous had collected in her nose in the few seconds she'd been crying.

"I want a tissue, please."

"Here you go, Dorit," I would reply.

"You do it! You do it!"

"Dorit." I've come to believe that my children thought the crying and resulting mucous and tears would bring us closer. Something about my having to clean their noses and cheeks would strengthen our relationship, maybe? As if this were a special experience for me.

"You do it, please, Daddy?"

"Okay, Dorit."

After we had dispensed with the tissues, I would sit down on the floor next to Lucas's bed. Lucas had always been anxious about going to sleep at night, and much of my focus was on trying to prevent his anxiety from growing. After I was settled, Dorit would snuggle into my lap and Lucas would either sit next to me on the floor or lie in his bed.

After I finished the last book, I would announce, "Time to get into bed, guys," as if they didn't already know what came next. This was the third transition, and to make it a bit easier on them and more enjoyable for me, I would give them a Special Daddy Hug, or what my children call the Los Tres Amigos Hug. The hug was one way I reminded myself that this time was special, and it made the whole experience less stressful. At one point I'd realized that I'd been thinking of this nightly ritual as a chore and was missing out on the fun of it.

Dorit made this transition challenging as well. She would often wander around the room or make a fuss over ensuring Lucas was settled in his bed—anything to not get into her bed.

"Dorit, please get into your bed."

"I'm going, Daddy," she would say, playing with her blankets and the 4,376 stuffed animals she had on her bed. But she wouldn't actually get in the bed. Meanwhile, Lucas would be in bed, his anxiety rising. It was the fourth transition of the evening that caused him stress, and waiting for it to happen only produced more anxiety in him.

Dorit would finally jump into bed and lie down, where she'd continue playing with her animals, calming herself down and preparing for sleep. If I had left the room at this point, Dorit would have fallen asleep on her own. But not Lucas.

So, I would kneel next to his bed, lean my arms on it, and ask him the same question I asked him every single night.

"What are your happy thoughts, Lucas?" In the past, I'd asked a number of follow-up questions about all of the "happy" things in his life, but this seemed to drag out the inevitable.

"Mommy and Daddy."

"What else?"

"Mommy Daddy. Mommy Daddy. Mommy Daddy."

"What else, Lucas?"

"Mommy Daddy. Mommy Daddy. Mommy Daddy." I think he thought this was funny, but it didn't seem to help him think about the things that lessened the anxiety he felt every night before going to sleep.

"So much I love you, Lucas," I reminded him, and gave him a couple of kisses on his head and cheek, beaming. I had tried a couple of ways to tell him I loved him at night, and this one did something for us both.

"So much I love you, too," he would reply, warming my heart. This really could be such a special experience.

I would smile at him once again and let him know I'd be right back. Then I would crawl over to Dorit's bed and start the process with her.

"What's in your bag of magic tricks, Dorit?"

One summer, my kids started getting scared at night, especially Lucas, and wouldn't go to sleep. I came up with the idea of a bag of magic tricks filled with happy things that they could use to feel better and go back to sleep when they felt scared. Dorit liked the full bag of magic tricks, but Lucas preferred to stick to the happy thoughts.

"Daddy," she said.

"But Daddy is my happy thought!" Lucas exclaimed.

"We can both have the same happy thought," she told him, before I could jump in and say the same thing.

"What else, Dorit?"

"Mommy."

"Daddy, I don't want to go to sleep," Lucas said, to make sure I remembered how close this all was to coming unglued.

"I know, Lucas, but it will be okay. You'll think about your happy thoughts."

This was the beginning of the fourth and final transition of our nightly ritual, the easiest for Dorit but the most difficult for Lucas. It was the time I turned out the light and walked out the door.

"I'm starting Enya over from the beginning," I informed them.

I stood with my hand on the light switch and looked at Lucas, trying to determine if he was going to be okay or not. I reminded them that I loved them. But before I could turn the light off, Dorit asked me a question.

"Happy announcement? Can you do happy announcement, Daddy?"

I paused.

If handled well, this could help them fall asleep peacefully, but if not? Disaster. Was this a delay tactic? Would it help her but make him more anxious? I had no idea.

I stayed silent.

Then I saw that Lucas was looking up at me with hope. He wanted to hear happy announcement, too, and so I made the decision.

"Okay, but after this it's time to go to sleep. Okay?"

"Okay."

"Okay."

I stood between their beds, so they both could see me, and read their birth announcement, which was hanging on the wall. I looked at their two little faces in the picture and marveled at how far we'd come already. It was the announcement I had written almost three years earlier:

> We are proud to share with you
> That our babies came by two
> One a girl, one a boy
> Bringing us double the joy

I read their names and their birthday, and my name and Gem's, and then I turned off the reading light and quietly crept across the room. I blindly reached out for the doorknob, opened the door, and stepped outside before closing it quietly behind me.

Not a sound.

If there was a problem, it would already have started by this point. I tiptoed down the stairs, trying to avoid the wood that creaked, to find Gem in the basement, our entertainment room, where we relaxed after our children went to bed. I checked the monitor and heard only the music and voice of Enya.

They were quiet.

Finally, my day was over and I could relax in the knowledge that I had done everything I could to be a good father that day.

Of course, tomorrow was only a few hours away.

## The Benefit of Losing Sleep

My heart ached. I had just put my twins (two and a half years old at the time) to bed. They weren't screaming or crying or calling my name. No, my beautiful children were falling asleep silently. While I felt a tremendous sense of pride—considering everything I'd been through in the couple of months leading up to this night, trying to get them to fall asleep in their beds on their own—I was also sad. This was my favorite part of the day and it was over too quickly. Just when my children were their most delicious, I found myself having to leave them. A part of me didn't want to walk out the door; a part of me missed hearing my boy say he didn't want me to leave, missed my girl's needing me to calm her down, missed hearing that they wanted me to lie down with them while they asleep.

After we went on vacation, my children—particularly Lucas—had started having a lot of trouble sleeping at night. This meant, of course, that my wife and I had also been having trouble sleeping at night. And in the exhausting struggle to help them fall asleep on their own, I reached a new level of closeness with my children that made me sort of miss the sleepless nights of crying and screaming. Sort of.

The first two weeks after our vacation went like this: Lucas would wake up in the middle of the night and call out for me, and I would go upstairs right away, hoping he wouldn't wake up my wife or his sister.

"What's wrong, Lucas?" I would whisper as I crept into the room.

"I'm a-scared," he'd say, making sure I knew he was both afraid and scared. "I'm a-scared, Daddy."

"Did you have a bad dream?"

"Yeah." He'd sigh.

"It's okay, Lucas. Why don't we just lie down and try to go back to sleep."

"I don't want to leave, Daddy. I don't want to leave."

"Okay, Lucas, I won't leave until you fall asleep."

"I don't want to leave, Daddy," he would whisper as he put his head back down and tried to fall back to sleep, hoping he wouldn't be frightened by what he saw. I hoped for exactly the same thing. Those first few nights, his falling back asleep could easily take an hour.

But these interactions really seemed to help him feel better, and soon he was waking up only once a night. I think part of what made us closer throughout this time was the fact that when he called out for me, I came to him. He could depend on me at night even though I wasn't around during the day. While being woken up at night was truly exhausting, there was something so special about hearing him call out for me to help, and about being able to provide comfort and safety for him.

What was most worrisome was that he truly seemed terrified at the notion of going to sleep. What could be haunting my little boy so badly? Neither of us had an answer and we felt helpless. While he felt better when I was in the room with him, it only seemed to reinforce his fear of being by himself. One night as I was putting him to bed, I told him I used to be scared to go to sleep.

"Yeah," he replied curiously.

"Yeah, really. When I was a kid I used to be scared to go to sleep," I whispered into his ear.

It was dark, but I could see him looking at me very intently, as if asking with his eyes, "Could it really be possible for Daddy to be scared?"

"You know what I used to do to help me fall asleep at night when I was scared?"

"Yeah." He always said "yeah" when I asked him if he knew something. I think he thought that I was asking if he wanted to know.

"I used to lie in my bed and imagine I was playing a game of baseball."

"Yeah," he said, exhaling.

"Yeah, and it always helped me fall asleep. That was my happy thought. What is your happy thought, Lucas? What's one thing or person that makes you happy?"

"Tita," he replied, meaning Tia (Aunt) Maria, my wife's sister. I had no idea that this innocent exchange would be the basis for my children's sleeping through the night once again. I had no idea I'd accidentally stumbled onto one of the things that would really make a difference for him. Fortunately, I was quick to pick up on the fact it was working. Soon I was asking him about his happy thought before he went to sleep every night.

"What's your happy thought, Lucas?"

No response.

"It's Tita, isn't it? You have so much fun with Tia, right?"

"Yeah."

Then I was asking him about his happy place (going to Friendly's to have ice cream and get balloons—he really is my boy).

For several more nights before he went to sleep and when he woke up in the middle of the night, I would ask him about all of his happy things.

"I'm a-scared, Daddy."

"I know. What do you do when you're scared, Lucas?"

"Happy thought!" he would reply immediately.

"Yeah, Lucas! Your happy thought! What else?"

"Happy place!"

"Good, Lucas!"

I don't know whether it was the distraction, his actually thinking about these happy thoughts, or simply our exchange, but it calmed him down, and when he was calm it was much easier for him to go back to sleep.

Then it was time to ask Lucas about his bag of magic tricks every night before he went to sleep. This bag of magic tricks was full of things he could think about whenever he got upset or scared, including his happy thought, his happy place, his happy song, his happy book, his happy family, his happy people (he came up with that one on his own), and every other happy thing that had happened in the past day or two or that was going to happen in the next day or so. Lucas was developing the tools he needed to get some control over his fear. And when I asked him about his bag of magic tricks every night, his face would glow. Not only did the contents of his bag of magic tricks make him feel better, but they became, I think, reminders of our special relationship. We, Daddy and son together, had created our own magic trick, our own happy thought, our own special connection.

Within another week of this process, Lucas was sleeping through the night more often than not. And he was going to sleep much more quickly and easily every night.

And then came the night when, after I'd tucked both of my children in and talked about their bags of magic tricks and how much I loved them, I turned off the light, walked out the door, and held my breath.

"Daddy?"

I didn't move. I didn't let out my breath. I waited for another word from the other side of the door, but it didn't come. I quietly walked downstairs and found Gem. She turned on the monitor and there was nothing but the comforting hum of the air conditioner. It was over. Our children were sleeping well once again. Even though the process had been extraordinarily challenging, I'm not sure if Lucas and I would've bonded like this in a different situation.

One night just before he fell asleep, I knelt down by the side of his bed and looked at him. And smiled. Lying on his back with his head turned so he could see me, he smiled back. He knew what was coming and he couldn't wait.

"What's in your bag of magic tricks tonight, Lucas?"

"Mommy and Daddy," he replied with a smile.

"What else?"

As he responded, I knew that the idea of happy thoughts and other happy things definitely helped, but there was more to it than that. What he and I did, the closeness we had developed through this nightly tradition, was what really made a difference. He was still scared to go to sleep, but finally he had some positive associations with it as well. And because of that, so did I.

I left as quietly as I could, feeling so proud of him and even of myself for the role I had played in helping him sleep well again. But as I went down to the basement to see my wife, I felt that pain in my chest. A pain not physical but emotional. A dark cloud that refused to be burned off by the hot sun. This ache came from the realization that it was my closeness with my son that was allowing him to sleep through the night, that was allowing him to not need me as much anymore. The ache was made worse by the knowledge that this was only the beginning; my little boy would start needing me less and less. But for the time being, I decided, I was going to bask in the glory of what we did have, of what we had created together, and of what couldn't be taken from us.

What was in my bag of magic tricks? What was my happy thought?

My special connection with my children.

## My Little Indulgence

The tricky part was the hallway—I would carefully place my foot on the wood floor in the tiny spots that didn't creak. Then I would gently place my hand on the doorknob and open the door without letting go, because if I did, it would slam into the wall. And then I would look into the room and bask in the sweetness of my five-year-old twins sleeping silently, peacefully, infusing my heart and soul with love, affection, and utter goodness.

That was my little indulgence for a long time.

Looking in on my sleeping children was like treating myself to dark chocolate in the afternoon of a tough day at the office. It lasted only ninety seconds, but the time was special.

I only started granting myself this indulgence when my children were around four years old. Other parents have told me stories about sneaking into their babies' rooms to watch them sleep, and I've never understood how they do it. For what felt like forever, our children were awfully light sleepers, and if Gem and I even got near their room they would wake up. To complicate things even more, for about three years, our children slept on a completely different floor from us, so it wasn't in the least practical to check on them. We relied entirely on a monitor to let us know whether they were sleeping or not. I've always believed some of the romance of listening to our children's sleeping was lost due to the monitor's buzzing.

But when they were five, Gem and I took them on our biannual trip to Ecuador (Gem was born there) and slept in the same room with them. We would put them to bed and leave the room to spend time with Gem's family before going to sleep ourselves. We were so worried about whether our children would be able to sleep with us in the same room—especially if we went to sleep at a different time. But every time we entered the room, we marveled at how peacefully they were sleeping. They were so delicate, precious, adorable—every single good feeling I had for them was reflected back to me. It was delicious, and I was awed by how much I enjoyed it, by how it helped right my orientation, my perspective on the world and my family. In essence, seeing my children sleeping was like an anchor, grounding me in the place I wanted to be, in the person I wanted to be: their daddy.

Around the same time as that trip, we moved to a different house. Instead of sleeping on different floors, we were now sleeping in rooms right across the hall from each other. So before I went to sleep at night, it was easy for me to take a little peek into their room, to see how they were sleeping, to renew my sense of what was good in my life—to see only the good in my children, in my life.

That was my little indulgence.

## Saying No for Her Own Good

"Can I sleep with you, Daddy?" my little girl asked me, oh so sweetly.

There it was, at 5:07 in the morning, the question I'd always dreaded.

How should a parent answer that question? Is it an immediate yes? Does it depend on the reason why she's asking? Is it a no?

Dorit, who was seven years old at the time, had been coughing all night long, struggling to sleep. Sometimes mucous pours down her throat and she chokes on it. Normally, she can sleep through it, but that night was really tough and she just couldn't sleep, no matter what I did. We'd been up for the past two hours and were both tired and frustrated.

As the Night Watchman, I always tried to get her and Lucas to go back to sleep in their own beds. I soothed them. I held them. I caressed them and cuddled them and made sure they knew I loved them. I'd like to think I made them feel better.

But I never let them into my bed.

I've always believed in the importance of a clear boundary between my marriage and my relationship with my children. If my wife and I are good together, if our marriage is strong, if our foundation is solid, then our family will be healthier. If our marriage isn't strong, everything else becomes significantly more difficult.

I've also always believed that it's a slippery slope: if I let them sleep with us one night, how could I tell them they couldn't the next night? How was I going to get them out of our bed at some point? When would my wife and I have time together, alone, just us?

I'm always surprised by some of the looks I get from other parents—especially mothers—when I tell them this. Shock. Disgust. How selfish could I possibly be? What about the well-being of my children? Don't I love them? Don't I want them to feel better?

I love my kids more than I ever dreamed possible. And I want them to be the healthiest they can be in terms of emotional maturity, independence, and self-confidence. If I can model for them how to soothe themselves, show them how to think their happy thoughts, how to think of all the people who love them, how to use their imaginations to calm themselves to sleep, if I can help them get more comfortable in bed so they can fall asleep, then I'm doing something for them that may very well last them a lifetime: I'm giving them the ability to care for themselves, to treat themselves the way they deserve to be treated, rather than showing them that they need to rely on someone else to do it for them.

"Can I sleep with you, Daddy?"

"No, Sweetie Girl. But how about if I help you get comfortable in your bed and see if we can get you some more sleep before morning?"

"Okay, Daddy."

We hugged and I tucked her back into bed after arranging her pillows. She fell asleep.

For two more hours. And Gem got to sleep for two more hours, as well.

Did my little girl feel unloved because I said no? I don't think so. And we all got our rest.

In the moment, it was almost painful to tell her no, but I still believe that it wasn't just a good decision then—it was a decision that will help my kids far into the future.

# Chapter Four

# I Don't Want to Go, but I Have to Leave

*For me, the hardest part about being a daddy was leaving my family every morning to go to work. I was going somewhere I didn't want to go, leaving the place where I felt comfortable, safe, and loved. My leaving was hard on my kids at various times as well. We came up with some creative ways to minimize that impact (and my guilt), but the reality was that I was leaving them every morning and none of us were happy about it.*

## Morning Anxiety

"Get up? Get up."

I knew that voice. It wasn't the first time it had woken me. It wouldn't be the last, I was sure.

"Get up!" my son said again.

"Mommeeeee," my daughter chimed in.

"Daddeeeeee," they whined in unison. There was no way they were going back to sleep. I looked at the clock.

5:28 a.m.

"You want to split up?" Gem asked. This was one of the ways we tried to get our two-year-olds back to sleep. She took one and I took the other into separate rooms and hoped they would go back to sleep. I didn't think it was likely on this particular morning.

"I'll get them," I told her. She didn't argue, knowing this meant she'd get an extra hour and a half of sleep.

By the time I got upstairs and opened their door, they were both standing up in their cribs and crying loudly. I picked up Dorit first and then went to Lucas's crib. When I had them both in my arms, I sat down on their couch and realized that Lucas was holding his woobie and Dorit was holding her Elmo and her doll, which she had named Dorit. They were definitely upset, but I had no idea why.

I kissed their cheeks, tasting salt, and asked them what was wrong. But they didn't have an answer for me.

"Do you want to lie down?" I asked, hoping they would want to go back to sleep. Immediately Lucas lay down next to me and Dorit lay down on top of me.

Until she realized we didn't have a blanket.

"A blanket, Daddy? A blanket?"

The only way to get a blanket was to disturb them. After I got it, Dorit got back into position on top of me, but Lucas was now sitting up.

I leaned back for a couple of minutes hoping he'd lie down again, but to no avail.

Realizing this wasn't working, I asked, "Do you want to make a bed on the floor and lie down with Daddy?"

"Sleep with Daddy?" my little girl asked.

"Sleep with Daddy?" my little boy echoed.

"Yes," I said, feeling as if maybe they finally understood what I was doing up there in their room. "Sleep with Daddy."

I laid the comforter on the floor and grabbed some pillows (can you tell this wasn't the first time I'd had to do this?), and we made ourselves comfortable on the floor. As usual, Dorit fell right to sleep. As usual, Lucas didn't.

At one point, when I thought Lucas was close to sleep again, I closed my eyes, let myself relax, and wondered if I might even get a little more sleep. Wishful thinking.

"Get down … boogie woogie woogie …"

Oh no.

"Who sings that, Daddy? Who sings that?" he asked loudly. Dorit stirred next to me.

"I don't know, Lucas," I whispered. I had no idea who sang that song and at that moment really couldn't have cared less. I just wanted him to sleep and not to wake Dorit.

"Mommy sings it, Daddy," he replied in his regular voice, which sounded boomingly loud.

"That's right, Lucas. Mommy does sing that song," I whispered, wishing she'd never taught him that one. Sleep wasn't going to happen. As if sensing that realization, my little girl popped her head up from underneath the blanket. Apparently, I was the only one not ready to be awake.

"Go downstairs with me?"

"Downstairs with Daddy?"

Since Dorit had already climbed on top of me, I picked her up first. Lucas held out his hand so I could hold it while I carried Dorit down the stairs. I stood up and off we went, with Elmo and Lucas's woobie, too.

When we got downstairs, I sat them on the couch. "What do you want to watch?"

"*Baby Beethoven*?" Lucas requested. He might have been the biggest Baby Einstein fan of all time. "*Baby Beethoven*?" he repeated. Who was I to argue? Especially at 6:15 in the morning, when I'd already been up for almost an hour.

I lay down on the couch, once again wishfully thinking I might get a little more sleep before the morning would officially have to start.

"Milk, Daddy? Cereal?" Usually my kids started every morning with milk in their sippy cups. And on those rare occasions when they woke before I left for work, they usually wanted to eat my cereal with me. Dorit was already excited about this opportunity. She was standing by the gate between the kitchen and the dining room–living room area, waiting. I left them watching *Baby Beethoven* while I went to get their sippy cups ready and make my cereal.

When I came back from the kitchen, Dorit asked, "On the couch?"

"Sure, Sweetie Girl. We can eat my cereal on the couch together."

I sat down and Dorit was immediately at my legs, looking into my bowl, waiting. But she's not that patient. "I want some."

"What?"

"I want some … please."

"Good." I'm never too tired to be a stickler for manners. I figure if they're going to eat half of my breakfast, the least they can do is ask nicely.

During this exchange, Lucas had climbed onto my back, something he rarely does.

"Would you like some, Lucas?"

"Yeah." How quickly they forget.

"What?"

"Yes, please."

"That's better, Lucas. Here you go." I'd be lucky if I got to eat half.

After they finished my cereal, we could hear Gem moving around.

"Where's Mommy?" Lucas asked.

"Mommy is getting dressed so she can come out and spend time with Lucas and Dorit."

"Spend time with Daddy?" he asked. I felt that twinge of guilt. Most mornings it was just a low hum. I'd learned to ignore it. But this morning was different.

"Daddy has to go to work today, Lucas."

He screamed in response. I reached out to give him a hug, but he moved away. Just then my wife walked in, and he ran to her. They left so she could change his diaper, which I had failed to do earlier in my sleepy state, and I scrambled to finish getting ready to leave.

When I started to give Dorit my usual hug and kiss goodbye, she started to get upset, too. For quite a long time, they'd gotten upset every morning when I left for work—especially Lucas. But we'd figured out some ways to make it easier for them and hadn't had any problems in the morning for a while. It's amazing how quickly and strongly my feelings of guilt came roaring back. I certainly hadn't missed them.

"Read. Read!" she screamed, handing me books. "Read!"

"Dorit, I want to read, but I have to go to work."

"NO, Daddy. Read!"

I was caught off guard by her outburst and began losing my patience. I didn't want to go. I'd rather be home with them.

"I need to go to work," I said, picking her up, "but I'll be home in time for our special Shabbat dinner."

"Oooohhh," she said, and then I knew she was going to be fine. Whenever her emotions were escalating into a tantrum, it seemed she was looking for a way to stop them but couldn't do it herself yet. When Gem and I were able to distract her with something she was excited about, she would say, "Oooohhh," and calm down. It was rather incredible because immediately afterwards, she'd have a smile on her face but tears streaming down her cheeks. I told her how much I loved her, gave her another hug and kiss, and put her down on the couch. She returned to watching *Baby Einstein*.

I said goodbye to Lucas as Gem was changing him, and he got a little upset again but seemed better. Then he hit his mother. I knew right away that he'd hit her because he was mad that I was leaving and this was the only way he knew how to express it. He'd hit Gem on her shoulder, but I felt as though he'd hit me right in the chest.

I told him not to hit, gave him another hug and kiss, and told him how much I loved him. Then I put my jacket on, grabbed my stuff, and walked out the door.

As I was closing the door, I heard my little boy asking, "Daddy, where are you? Daddy, where are you?"

I closed my eyes as I closed the door.

I got into my car and drove to the train station with a heavy, achy feeling in my heart and stomach. When I parked the car and got out, I found myself blinking away tears—tears the cold morning wind only made worse.

**Big Brown Eyes Looking Up at Me**

When my twins were nineteen months old, I was in the habit of getting up early to ride my bike. I'd arrive back home in time to shower and get dressed before they woke up. The morning provided some of the few moments I got with my children during the week. And Gem got a few precious extra minutes of sleep before spending all day with them by herself.

Once they were up, I had to eat my breakfast, get their milk, and do all the other things I needed to do to get out of the house on time. So while it was special time, it could also be stressful time. Even after Gem woke up, it was still pretty hectic; when she came into the playroom, I usually rushed off to take my vitamins and brush my teeth. After a minute or so I would see the face of my little boy looking up at me—he wanted to watch Daddy.

I'm embarrassed to say that my initial reaction to this was annoyance. I was in a rush and doing everything I could to get out of the house on time to catch my train, and his presence impeded that process. When you have two toddlers, you lose time as well as any semblance of privacy. If I just tried to do what I had to do, I would find myself constantly trying to avoid tripping over him. If I picked him up and took him to his mother, he would show up outside the bathroom door again a minute later, depending on how long it had taken to wriggle out of Mommy's arms. But one day it hit me. He wasn't trying to be annoying; he was trying to learn how to be just like Daddy, just like me.

After kicking myself for being an idiot, I examined the potential to capture a few extra moments with Lucas each morning. Here was my little boy, looking to me, fascinated by the things I did because he wanted to be just like Daddy. I was overwhelmed by a combination of terror and joy. Lucas had no idea of the mistakes I made every day, had no idea I was just an average guy making my way through life. And he didn't care whether I felt worthy enough to be his role model. It was too late. I already was.

So, my morning routine changed. When I took my vitamins, I'd help him take his, too. After I finished brushing my teeth and rinsing my mouth,

I would help him rinse his mouth and wipe it with my towel. He absolutely loved it. After I brushed my hair, he wanted to do the same and would walk around carrying a brush the size of his head, trying to use it. Utterly adorable. Not surprisingly, my relationship with Lucas became stronger than ever.

I still wonder: Did he understand on some level that I'm male and he is too? Was that why he watched me so intently while my daughter didn't? What was he thinking about while he watched? Was I doing enough for him, enabling him to feel the same strong connection I felt with him? I certainly hope so. I have learned, though, that there are times when it's better to ask fewer questions when it comes to being a parent.

I came to look forward to my son's presence during my morning grooming. While brushing my teeth, I would look for him, waiting to hear the little patter of his feet, waiting to see his beautiful brown eyes staring up, waiting for him to be right behind me.

**Making It Easier**

You know how some parents look forward to going back to work to get a break from their children and spouses? I'm not one of them. I hate going to work in the morning. Absolutely hate it. I hate leaving my family, especially on Mondays, after I've spent so much time with them during the weekend.

It was especially bad when my children were nineteen months old. They hated it, too. Sometimes they would cry and scream when I leaned down to say goodbye. Other times they clung to me and refused to let go—as if I really wanted to leave them in the first place.

My children developed different ways of dealing with my leaving in the morning. Dorit somehow learned on her own how to keep her connection to me throughout the day. Gem told me she would point to pictures of me and yell out, "Da-Dee!" Or (and this just broke my heart) she would pick up my sneakers, take them to Gem, and say, "Da-Dee shoes." When she started to do this, my leaving in the morning wasn't as hard on either of us.

But my leaving was much harder on Lucas. When he gets excited, he sometimes has to back away from what has got him so excited; his whole body shakes with emotion. Even as a baby, he was quite attuned to his emotions; he just didn't have the tools to deal with them yet. To deal with my leaving, he would cry or scream or remain distant. When I came home at night, he would barely acknowledge me, while his sister would scream out "Daddy!" and lift her arms for me to pick her up. This hurt, and also made me angry—mostly at myself. I hated how much I was hurting Lucas every morning.

This continued until Gem observed that Dorit was finding ways to remain connected to me during the day and Lucas wasn't. The challenge became a matter of how to help Lucas do the same.

Maybe a piece of clothing? One of my shirts, perhaps? I spent time during my lunch hour looking around in different stores, trying to find something that might better tie us together in his mind. While trying to find a long-term solution, I decided to give him the towel I used when I rode my bike in the morning. Giving him a hug and a kiss while leaving one morning, I asked him to take care of it for me during the day.

The second day I gave it to him, he said, "Tow-a?" The third day, Gem told me that he'd been in our bedroom and had found one of my work shirts on the floor. He lay down, put his head on it, and said, "Da-Dee." He got it! He'd connected to me while I wasn't there. Tears filled my eyes.

A few weeks later, he was reaching out for the towel in the morning because he couldn't wait to hold it. During the day, he would try to put it on his shoulder and wear it the way I did. Not only did he no longer get upset when I left, he and his sister also waved "bye, bye" to me as I drove in front of the house on my way to work.

As for me, I have pictures of them all over my wall and a slideshow of them as my screensaver—my ways of keeping that connection to them during the day so I don't get too upset.

**When They Give Back to Me**

Gem picked me up at the train station. It had been a tough day. We hugged and I never wanted to let go. I never feel safer than I do when I'm in her arms.

She had yoga and a school meeting that evening though, so it was Los Tres Amigos time, and I was momentarily very concerned. I didn't feel I was in the right frame of mind to be a good Daddy, plus I was feeling sick to my stomach. We ended up going to McDonald's, where the kids had Happy Meals and I couldn't eat anything at all. I had already decided that it was a good night to be a bit more lenient. Sometimes I'd get so lost in the little things that I'd put myself (and them) in a bad (or even worse) mood, and then we'd have no fun at all. We had a nice chat and they behaved very well (maybe sensing I was not in such a good mood). At one point, Dorit—who seemed as if she'd been missing her daddy the past couple of days—got down from the table and came over to give me a hug.

"I love you, Daddy."

"I love you, too, Sweetie Girl."

I held on to her for as long as she'd let me, and when I looked up I saw an older man sitting at a table near us. He smiled, having seen my moment with my little girl. I couldn't help but smile as well.

That night, we were early starting our bedtime ritual, so I picked two fairly long books to read them: *The Three Little Pigs* (for the first time) and *The Cat in the Hat* (I'm a big Dr. Seuss fan). Somehow I found it in me to act out the characters, using different voices for the cat, the fish, and the little boy, which obviously made the experience much more enjoyable for my children (and for me, too, even though I constantly changed the voices because I forgot what I was doing). Reading those books consumed almost twenty minutes, and my kids were captivated. It was awesome.

Then I tickled them and tickled them. And then I tickled them some more. Their laughter was like a magical healing potion, covering my body with good feelings, with love. It seeped into my soul, where it had been so dark for far too long. After I read them their Paddington Bear book (our regular right-before-bed story), I tickled them some more.

It was truly a wonderful way to end what had been a terrible day.

As I was tucking them in and going through their happy thoughts, Lucas said, "And Daddy?"

When I looked at him, he blew me a kiss and then put his head back down on the pillow.

I blew him a kiss right back and walked out the door. I remember walking down the stairs that night and marveling that I had missed something. I'd been spending so much time thinking about all that I needed to be for my children, about the things I needed to teach them, about how I needed to be there when they needed me, to make sure they knew and felt how much I loved them. But that night, I began to realize they were becoming their own people, able to give back to me when I actually needed a little.

**Work Friends**

The question had come up a couple of times. It was gnawing at me. Finally, it was unavoidable.

"You going to see your work friends?" It gave me pause. I had enough guilt about leaving them every morning—the last thing I wanted them thinking was that I left because I was going to hang out with some friends, that hanging out with friends every day was more important than being with my three-year-old children.

I knew they didn't really understand what work was. To them, it was simply the place Daddy went to every day. But they knew what friends were; they had a few themselves. They went to friends' houses to play and have fun. I certainly didn't want them feeling that's what I was doing without them every day. On the other hand, I didn't want them thinking that work was something tortuous and painful. There had to be some balance.

Then they went one step further. Lucas was talking on one of his toy phones. He handed it to me, saying, "It's your work friends." Now, I'd never received a phone call at home from work, and I had never called work from home.

"Tell them I can't talk right now because I'm with my children," I told him, not sure what to do.

Taking back the phone, he said, "He can't talk. He's with us." Then he turned to Dorit. "You want to talk to his work friends?"

"What are their names?" she asked. Lucas said my boss's name and my cubemate's name. (Children really do hear everything we say, even when we're not talking to them.)

I was a bit flummoxed by the whole situation. The "work friends" concept was building momentum, and something about it felt wrong. My children seemed to be developing an idea of where I went during the day, away from them, that was more concrete than the abstract concept of work. And it seemed to be an image I didn't want them to have.

I talked to Gem about it and she made a good suggestion: I needed to talk more about what I did during the day in very simple terms, to help them build a more accurate image in their minds.

This wasn't the most important situation I was dealing with in terms of trying to be a good father, but it was one that had caught me by surprise and had me questioning what I really wanted my children thinking I did all day.

Because of that "phone call," I made more of an effort to share with my children what I did during the day—the things I worked on, the stories I wrote, and the people I helped. I also took them to my office a few times a year so they could picture it and meet the people I talked about. That probably helped more than anything, and they always got excited about visiting.

And I also spent time making sure they knew how much I enjoyed being with them, that I wasn't choosing work over being with them. I have work friends, but they are not the same as my family.

**Because I Don't See You**

"I'm NOT crying," my almost-three-year-old little girl said to me while I was cleaning her hands after our messy dinner of spaghetti and meatballs. I hadn't thought she was crying. So why had she said that? Was this one of those toddler things that just didn't make any sense? Or was she telling me something important?

I decided to explore, just in case. "Do you feel like crying, Dorit?" I asked, continuing to focus on cleaning her hands and face.

"No."

*Phew.*

Okay, then. That settled that.

"But I'm a little bit grumpy," she added. I immediately looked at her beautiful face.

*Uh-oh.*

"Oh, Sweetie Girl, why are you grumpy?" I was following her lead now.

"Because I don't see you."

*I knew it.*

I leaned closer and stopped cleaning her hands.

"Because I don't see you in the morning." And just like that I was on my knees both physically and emotionally.

*It does hurt them. I knew it.*

"You know when I don't see you in the morning, I really miss you, right?" I said. "You know I miss you?"

"Yes," she said.

Then the moment was over, and like a baseball player shaking off a brushback pitch, she shook it off and was lost in playing with her twin brother and Mommy.

But twenty-four hours later I still hadn't shaken it off.

As I've written about, the mornings were a challenging yet crucial time with my children. On the mornings when they woke up and I was still home, their first question was, "Do you have to go to work, Daddy?"

"Yes, I do," I would say with resignation. I was the sole breadwinner. Gem cared for them all day. That was our deal. So I had to leave.

To be honest, though, it was more than that. I didn't earn the money in our family only because of our deal. I left every morning because that's what my father had done. It was the main thing I'd learned from my father about being a father. But he'd never gotten the balance right, and we'd never had much of a connection, much of a relationship, a sense of closeness. I desperately wanted that closeness with my children, and going to work every day scared me because it got in the way of that.

As summer turned to fall, it stayed dark in the morning, making it easier for my kids to sleep longer. Which then made it more likely I wouldn't see them in the morning. This was what Dorit was feeling. I didn't think it was one morning in particular that had upset her, but the accumulation of many mornings waking up to find her Daddy wasn't home. Our strong connection made this difficult for her. She was now old enough to be aware that she missed me, aware that I was somewhere else, not with her.

There were times when I'd come home and Dorit would be whiny or emotional and it turned out that she just needed some time with me. When I came home I would try to have at least a little time with each of my children, but with two it can be difficult to create special individual time; between dinner, bathtime, and nebulizing every night, there just weren't enough minutes.

When I left in the morning before they woke up, it was easy to fool myself into thinking it was better that way. Every time I had to say goodbye to them, I caused them pain. If I left before they woke up, no harm, no foul. But just because I didn't see it didn't mean it wasn't there. My children missed me every day I went to work, even though when I was around I tried to give them everything I had, everything I could to make up for my time away. I could only hope they'd understand this when they were older. Probably. It wasn't much solace at the time.

I'm feeling a bit grumpy myself.

**Sunday Sadness**

Sundays have always been a tough day for me. I'm a guy who struggles with living in the moment, and Sunday is the epitome of that struggle for me. Sunday means that tomorrow is Monday, which means that my weekend is over. And so, I get Sunday Sadness. This sadness, or maybe more appropriately, this mourning, is less about having to go to work and more about missing out on time with my wife and twins. I hate to see our weekends come to an end.

Ironically, though, weekends as a parent can be tough. Parenting is a muscle I use much more on the weekends, so by the time Monday rolls around I'm often exhausted. But it's my favorite time of the week, my favorite time in my life.

Weekends are when I get to spend real time with my children, when I get to make up for not being there the past week. Weekends are when they wake up and I'm still there. Weekends are when I make them my now-famous chocolate chocolate chip pancakes. Weekends are when we get to be Los Tres Amigos, the Three Friends, because Gem is either asleep or maybe out with her mother and sister taking some time for herself. Weekends are the only time I get to say "NO!" when they ask me if I have to go to work. "No, I'm staying home with my children!"

Weekends are also a chance to do the things we can't do during the week because of dinner, baths, medicine, and early bedtimes—a chance to do the special things that build memories for us. Dorit had been asking me to make a fire, something we just didn't have time for during the week. She asked me so nicely, so sweetly, that I knew I had to figure out a time to do it. The next Saturday night, we had a Pizza Hut picnic on the floor in front of a roaring fire that my children helped me build (they crumpled up the newspapers to get it started). We enjoyed the warmth, counted all of the colors, and had a relaxing (relative use of the word—it was still dinner and they were still twins) evening.

Weekends are a time for seeing my kids when they aren't tired from their day. One weekend, I found myself falling in love with Lucas over and over. He'd been having a rough time going to sleep at night—primarily because he missed me and would start screaming and banging on the door when I walked out of their room after tucking him in. But that weekend, he was just precious during the day: the way he held my hand to show me something, the way he exhibited his intelligence, which he was often too shy to do, the way he enjoyed listening to and singing along with music with his heart and soul, just like I do. He was absolutely delicious and I found myself wanting to savor every moment with him.

Monday morning means the end of that kind of family time for the week. But remembering how things are on the weekends helps keep me going during the week and rejuvenates me as a parent. My weekends are made up of those special moments that remind me of how lucky I am to have my life.

# Chapter Five

# Parents as Partners — Living, Loving, and Working Together

*I have never forgotten that my incredible family is a result of the relationship Gem and I have. We are the foundation for the love created in our family. Whenever we lost that connection, our whole family suffered; it didn't matter if we were great parents. But when Gem and I were doing well, everything in our lives, the happy chaos we experienced daily, was always better—for us and our okapis.*

## Parenting Is a Team Sport

"You do not speak to Daddy like that!" Gem scolded our four-year-old daughter. Dorit had just yelled at me out of anger, and that was not acceptable in our house. "Go to your time-out."

Dorit knew that screaming, especially at the dinner table, resulted in a time-out, but she didn't want to go. I sat watching my little girl figure out what her options really were. And while observing this, I was struck by something I have given a lot of thought to since. How often do you and your partner back each other up as parents?

There's no question in my mind now, after having twins, that parenting is a team sport—it works best if both parents use the same playbook. The strength of the players is revealed through how well they stick up for each other. Dorit had just broken two of our rules: show respect for your family members, especially your parents, and don't scream. And Gem had jumped in to back me up. I don't think she consciously made that decision; she did it because we work together that way, because she knows I would do the same for her.

For us, this has been the key to a true partnership. Backing each other up builds on the trust we've established and ensures that our children understand that these lines in the sand, these rules, these limits we set for them, are serious and there are consequences for crossing them.

There are two scenarios where it's very important that we back each other up as parents. The first, as in the example above, is when one of our children talks back or disrespects us.

The second revolves more around the child's behavior. One day I came home from work to find Gem telling Dorit to get into time-out (yes, she is much more the boundary tester). Dorit was not budging.

Before I'd even put my backpack down and taken off my jacket, I told Dorit to get into the time-out corner. Dorit looked at me, realized she was boxed in, and hung her head. Then she walked into time-out. I didn't need an explanation; if Gem was giving Dorit a time-out, then she needed a time-out. If I had come in and questioned what was going on, it would have sent the powerful message that I didn't think Gem could handle it herself, that she wasn't the authority on whether rules had been broken, and on the consequences for such actions.

Gem and I have talked about the rules we have in place, and have developed a set of expectations for our children. This understanding makes backing each other up much easier. If one of us has a problem with the way the other is handling a situation, we wait until we are alone and the situation is over. Then we talk about it, to see if next time there might be a better way to handle it or if we need to be more or less flexible with the rule.

"Okay, Dorit. Your time-out is over. Please say you're sorry to Daddy and come back to the table."

She apologized, gave me a delicious hug, and joined us again at the dinner table.

Our family started because Gem and I fell in love with each other. Our family doubled in size, but the core never changed; we're still in love and still respect each other after twenty-five years together. We hope that this trust we've built between us over the years will model trust for our children and they'll be able to build their own relationships like ours.

## The Relationship Richter Scale

Having children is like inviting an earthquake into your life. Seismologists measure the strength of an earthquake using the Richter scale. If there were a relationship Richter scale, having children would score a 9.1—a devastating blow to a relationship. In addition to the initial damage, aftershocks from this earthquake can continue for months and years. When a child is born, the tectonic plates of the relationship shift, and how they will eventually settle is anyone's guess.

Gem and I had been together for thirteen years by the time our twins were born. We'd been together through college, graduate school, and first jobs. We'd been through four countries and even a bloodless coup. We'd lived in four different homes in three cities. We'd been through several careers, unemployment, and my battle with anxiety and depression. But we'd gotten through it all because we'd always worked together as a team. When she got pregnant, we promised each other that no matter what, we would deal with this new journey as a team, just as we always had.

After the earthquake of our children's arrival, it took us fourteen months to reestablish our special connection—fourteen months of fights, silence, stress, and loneliness. Fourteen months of our identities as parents absolutely crushing our identities as husband and wife. It's amazing how easily it happened, how difficult this period was, and how long it took to undo the damage.

We had no idea how disruptive having a child, let alone two, would be. It's one of those things you can't understand until you experience it, and by then it's too late to turn back. Before our twins were born, we'd spent almost all of our spare time together; after, we had no spare time. Before, we'd tell each other all about our days; after, we only had the time and energy to tell each other that a baby needed to be changed or it was once again time to feed them. Before, we would go out to eat regularly; after, we were lucky if we ate regularly. I can't tell you how many times we fell asleep where we sat, each of us holding a sleeping baby, afraid to disturb them.

But it was more than the sleep deprivation and constant stress. I really missed the intimacy my wife and I had shared. Relationships are built on intimacy, time spent being physically and emotionally close to each other, sharing your heart, soul, and private thoughts. Forget about sex—neither of us had the energy (okay, I could've summoned the energy had there been an opportunity)—what we were really missing was intimacy, the closeness that had gotten us through every other earthquake we'd experienced. Before we had kids, when we woke up in the morning and before we went to sleep at night, we would spend at least a few minutes cuddling. But after, we rarely slept—alone or together. So it stopped happening. Without intimacy, we were just two people with a shared history dealing with the overwhelming responsibility of two babies in a one-bedroom apartment.

When we moved into our new house, things didn't get any better. While I left the house every day for a job that damaged my psyche, Gem spent every day with our children building closeness, intimacy. She nursed our children for fourteen months. She was building a strong bond with them, a bond I wanted them to have with her. I just didn't realize that this bond would come at the expense of my bond with her. When it was just the two of us, we shared intimacy only with each other. But now, she had a strong, intimate connection with our children, while I was feeling disconnected from her and them. I felt as if I were no longer a priority, and neither was our marriage, and that was a terrible blow. Before, when faced with earthquakes, we would stand together and face them. But this time, I seemed to be on the wrong side of the fault line, not sure how to get back to where my family was.

When we couldn't get them to sleep through the night, things only got more desperate. Not only did we go months without getting more than three or four hours of sleep in a row—and often no more than two—we also spent a couple of months sleeping in different rooms trying to get our children to sleep through the night and not wake each other up. Then there were the nights we spent sitting up in bed listening to at least one, if not both, of them screaming. We'd try to figure out how to handle it and often disagree. I fully understand why sleep deprivation is used as a tor-ture device. It was horrible. Even when we did sleep we were constantly on alert, scared one of them would start screaming, so sleep ceased to be restful. Our relationship became almost completely devoid of intimacy. We were no longer affectionate with each other; we barely hugged and kissed anymore. We were so beaten down from being parents, we had nothing left for each other as spouses.

When our children started sleeping through the night, things didn't automatically improve. Though we'd finally started to get some sleep, having lost the shelter of our intimacy, our arguments had become fre-quent and nasty. We filled the distance between us with insults, suspi-cion, and cruelty, destroying what little trust remained. When we couldn't find the baby monitor, finding it wasn't enough. We needed to know who was at fault for its not being in the right place. Soon, silence seemed the easier and safer solution and we only talked about baby stuff. It's amaz-ing how the momentum of a relationship can change. After thirteen years of mostly wonderful times, we had become a couple who looked forward to sleeping to get away from the tension and silence. I could see the path we were on and it was bleak. My life had lost its center of gravity, its foun-dation. I imagined what it would be like if we weren't together anymore and wondered how I would go on. But how long could we live like this?

The turning point came when Gem stopped nursing. All of a sudden she wasn't as tied to them. We could stay at a hotel one night and try sleeping in. She was no longer the key provider of nutrients for them, which meant she was less an extension of them and more her own person again. And her sex drive, which had diminished during nursing, began to return. Being able to spend a night away allowed us to really talk about our issues in a neutral environment where we weren't overly stressed out and were somewhat rested. Soon we were able to have open, honest conversations about where our marriage was and what we needed from each other.

One of the most important things I learned from the experience was that a big part of relationships is momentum. When things are going well, it's easy to see the positives. We filter everything our partner says through a positive lens, which prevents fights and makes your relationship even stronger. But when things are bad, the opposite happens. Every negative is highlighted and every word is seen through the lens of suspicion and anger. The earthquake of becoming parents to twins triggered the most overwhelming negative momentum we've ever experienced. But we've finally recovered from that major tectonic-plate shift. More importantly, it's now much easier for us to feel the rumblings of trouble long before they get serious. Gem and I make more of an effort to carve out time for ourselves, time for our relationship, whether that means having a special dinner after our kids are in bed or setting up sleepovers for the kids at the grandparents' house so we can have time together doing something fun, just the two of us. Knowing how to reverse negative momentum has made these last few years, despite the incredible difficulty of raising twins, the best we've had together.

## Concentrating on Us

Remember the game Concentration? You turn over one card and then have to remember where its match is. And if you forget, you lose your turn. By the time our children were two years old, I had come to feel as though my wife and I were playing that game all the time. Every time we picked up a card with a picture of our children, we could easily find the match. But when we picked up a picture of our relationship, we almost never remembered where the other card was and lost our turn. We had been doing a much better job of being parents than being married.

This is what drove us to finally get away for a weekend without our twin two-year-olds. We had done this once or twice before, but this time I was so nervous my stomach was bubbling. A complex concoction of emotions was coming to a boil.

Gem and I desperately needed the time. The first year after our twins' birth had been absolutely atrocious. The second year had definitely been an improvement, but we both knew we still weren't where we wanted to be. Our husband and wife roles had been crushed by our father and mother roles. This was a big reason we could never remember where the other relationship card was.

During the few months leading up to our weekend away, the good stretches started outnumbering the bad ones for the first time since our children were born. Building on this positive momentum, we had one of those groundbreaking talks where we were completely honest with each other about how we felt and what we wanted, and it went incredibly well. There was a lot riding on our getaway weekend. It would either solidify the progress we had made or demonstrate the weaknesses in the foundation we were trying to rebuild.

But by no means was that the only thing contributing to the chemical experiment being conducted in my stomach. As much as I knew that Gem and I needed to get away, I didn't want to leave my children. I was working full-time and saw them for such a small percentage of their waking hours during the week; weekends were when I tried to catch up on some of what I'd missed during the week. It was why, during weekends,

I still woke up early in the morning when they woke up, so I could have breakfast with them, just the three of us. I was torn because getting special time with my wife meant losing out on special time with my children. I felt so selfish. I knew that Gem and I needed to focus on our relationship so we wouldn't keep forgetting where the matching relationship card was; I just wished I didn't have to abandon my children to do it.

After we put them down to bed that Friday night, we said goodbye to Gem's mother, who was looking after them, and got into the car, where we heaved a collective sigh. We really were doing this, taking time away to be alone. I'd even made a new playlist for her on my iPod. The fact that we were driving to our weekend away was significant. My wife and I had fallen in love during road trips.

We met in college, Alfred University, a small school in western New York State. Frankly, there wasn't much to do up there, so Gem and I would often hop in the car, put on our favorite music, and just drive. We'd pick a direction and see where it took us. On these drives, we would talk and talk and talk. Especially at night, on quiet, dark roads, there was an intimacy in the car; a sense that we were the only ones in the world at that moment in time. That sense of isolated togetherness allowed us to truly get to know each other, hear the stories that had made us who we were and shaped our beliefs. This sharing created our own sense of history, though we had no idea that's what we were doing at the time.

We were thinking about all of this as we got onto the highway that Friday night, and I could feel the connection between us reestablishing itself, like octopi tentacles reaching out and finding each other. As we listened to the playlist I'd made her, we held hands.

We didn't get to the hotel until late that night, and we went right to sleep after we checked in. On Saturday morning, Gem woke up very concerned about our children—I hadn't even really thought of them. She called her mother and found out they had slept well and were doing great. And then she felt better, more relaxed, while I felt more tense. Was there something wrong with me because I hadn't been thinking about them? And now that I'd learned they were fine, I felt somewhat jolted out of my state of being with my wife. It was almost as if I'd jumped back into the husband role so completely that I'd forgotten my other role—father. It took some time before I could readjust.

On Sunday morning, I started feeling a low-level, anxious hum. I knew that Gem and I were doing really well. But that was the problem. Of course we could reestablish our connection without our children around, but what were we going to do once we returned home? I almost couldn't enjoy the time we were having, as I was too afraid of how hard it would be when we got home. Gem and I talked about this as well, but didn't really come up with any concrete solutions. We did promise each other, though, that we would try to get away more, and that we would make more of an effort to communicate when a problem started to arise, before it became too big to handle. Heading home, we once again felt a mixture of emotions. We wanted to get back to see our children, but we didn't want to lose what we had regained while away from them. The balance of our spousal and parental roles felt fragile.

Our twins were so excited to see us when we arrived, jumping up and down and giving us big hugs. It felt great to be home, but soon there was dinner to worry about, and getting them ready for bed—which was always a battle against time and two tired two-year-olds. My wife and I quickly switched into parent mode, and I already felt myself beginning to forget the things we had promised each other about maintaining our connection.

But then, just before bedtime, we all got on the couch and started reading their books in preparation for putting them into their cribs. Dorit was sitting on my lap, Lucas was sitting on Gem's lap, and my wife and I were sitting right next to each other, touching shoulders and legs. I looked over at her while our children were completely absorbed by one of the books, and she looked right at me. Her smile was dazzling, and there was a little twinkle in her eye—a look that said, in all this craziness, she loved me. I gave her the same look back without even realizing that the low-level, anxious hum had disappeared. We had found the matching relationship card and it was our turn once again.

## Mommy Do It

Few things haunt fathers more than the phrase "Mommy do it!" These words may be presented differently for each father, but the idea underpinning them is the same: "Mommy is better than you, Daddy." Every time my children said these words to me, they bounced around my brain in a mental pinball game, smashing into bumpers of doubt and low self-esteem, leaving me helplessly tilted.

Game over.

I lose.

When my children were born, I made a commitment to them and myself that I would do everything in my power to be around for as much of their lives as possible, to be as involved as possible. To be for them the father I'd never had. But, like many fathers, I'm riddled with doubts and self-confidence issues. Like many fathers, I don't have a role model to look up to or turn to with my questions. Like most fathers, I learned quickly: "Fake it until you make it." Now I'm more comfortable being a father than I've ever been. But the doubt, the self-questioning, has never gone away.

When my children were about two and a half years old, a disturbing trend made all of my doubts rise like an erupting volcano that threatened to destroy all of the work I'd done becoming a comfortable, confident father. Over and over again I heard the same phrases.

"Mommy do it?"

"Go with Mommy?"

"Where's Mommy?"

It didn't matter what I was doing or what the situation was. My children always wanted Mommy. One night, Gem and I walked into the house together and I couldn't even get a "Hello," let alone a kiss and hug from either of my children. It was as if I weren't even there. And it made me wonder why I was. Why was I working so hard to be there for my children if I seemingly had no impact on their lives? When Mommy was around, Daddy might as well not have been.

In my less self-punishing and self-pitying moments I could remember that there were a number of things going on. The biggest, most important variable was my wife. I couldn't have picked a better person to be the mother of my children. She loves them unconditionally, in ways I never even imagined were possible. At the time, she was with them all day, and I believe with every fiber of my being that as a result, my children have a foundation of love that will support them for the rest of their lives.

If you spent the day with the most loving person on the planet, why would you want to be with anyone else? Not only was being with Gem what they were used to, not only was it comfortable, but it also must've felt really good. Please don't get me wrong. She's not perfect, and I have some pretty great strengths. But the combination of her personality and their being with her almost every moment of every day since they were born made her almost the perfect parent for them. When she was around, I would often get the child who was too slow to ask for Mommy.

And so, her strong presence was precisely why the remedy to this situation had to involve both of us.

For our children to see and learn I could be there for them just as much as Gem was, they needed to experience my caring for them in the same way, meeting their most important needs.

That meant I sometimes needed to be alone with them; Gem needed to make herself absent to give me room to be more involved. We spent some time discussing things we could do and concluded that because I worked during the day, the biggest opportunity for change was bed time.

When I first started putting them to bed on my own, the kids really weren't happy about it. There was a lot of screaming for Mommy, but Gem would go downstairs, turn off the monitor, and relax in front of the TV, something she never got to do.

It took several days before our kids realized this was for real: Daddy was putting them to bed now. They started to warm up to the idea, and I knew we'd crossed a threshold when one day, Dorit took me by the hand, truly one of the most special things in the world, and said, "Ladybugs?"

"You want to look for ladybugs?"

"Yes. Let's go to the circus."

Apparently, the circus was where one found ladybugs. I had no idea. She led me around their bedroom until we got to a place where she saw ladybugs.

"Right der," she said in that toddler accent. We got down on the floor to have a closer look. "That's a big one. That's a big one."

"Yes it is," I replied. "How many spots does it have?"

"One … two … three … four … five … six … seveneightnineten!" They always had ten, by the way, no matter how big or small they were.

Then she stood up, held out her hand, and said, "Ladybugs?" With a huge grin on my face, I stood up, took her hand, and let her take me to the next ladybug location in the bedroom.

There was no missing Mommy. No crying out for her. Only spending time with Daddy, with me. Before I knew it, the twins were fighting to sit on my lap, snuggling up to me for stories, and wanting me to lift them up into bed.

I was able to prove to my children I could be there for them and take care of them. But it wouldn't have been possible if Gem and I hadn't had frank discussions about our roles as parents. Gem had to give up something special, but she also knew how important it was for me to have a special relationship with our kids, and that this relationship benefited me and them as well as her.

If my wife hadn't been so supportive of my building a strong relationship with our children, would it have happened? I've always wondered. But what I am certain of is that everything about parenting is easier when we work together.

## Building a Blueprint for Loving Together

I looked at my exhausted wife, and we smiled at each other and snuggled in to watch another episode of *Battlestar Galactica* (the remake). We'd recently celebrated twenty years of being together. I still marvel that we've made it this far. There is no one on this earth I love like I love my wife. She's the most amazing person I've ever met. But it hasn't been easy. Love is not enough to survive children.

The first eighteen months or so were horrible, the worst we've ever had. We completely lost our way, forgetting how to be husband and wife, how to be people not attached to children, how to be anything other than parents. We found our way again by taking time for ourselves, thanks to grandparents who love their grandchildren (and us, too).

Even though our children are older now, and things have never been as bad as those first eighteen months, maintaining a healthy relationship is still challenging. The chaos of our lives takes a toll on us; we come home from work almost too tired to carry on a conversation, days go by where we don't talk, the distance between us grows. As that distance grows, it feels harder to bridge it. It's easier to watch TV or go to bed.

In the movies, the story always ends when the people realize they're in love and finally get together, as if everything after that is easy. In real life, that's when the hard part begins. Being in love, keeping the love alive when work is stressful, the kids aren't behaving, and you're utterly drained, that's the challenge.

Both my parents and Gem's got divorced, so neither one of us has role models for a successful marriage. We're learning on the fly, trying to figure out what we want from a relationship and doing our best to make it happen. We hope we're building the blueprint we never had.

Gem and I love to cuddle on the couch and watch an episode of something on Netflix. Sometimes when things have been rough, we'll make sure the kids have dinner and then while one of us is putting them to bed, the other is picking up Indian or Thai food from one of our favorite places so we can treat ourselves to a special dinner in the middle of the week. We also make sure we have at least a couple of weekends a year (and even more nights) just the two of us, away from the stress and pressure of being at home.

But what has really helped is the way we stay in touch during the day, either through email or text messaging. We send each other friendly reminders of what needs to be done, interesting things to read, little love notes, or quotes from love songs—or we just plain check in with each other. The truth is, we're almost always on each other's minds, and sharing that with each other during the day when we're not together makes a difference. It's helped us to stay connected even when we're apart, making it a little bit easier to reconnect when we get home.

There's no question that this life—working, building a business, raising children, and trying to take care of ourselves—is extraordinarily challenging. But when Gem and I are together, when we're connected, every single thing in my life is easier. And I feel better. And we're better parents. And we're giving our okapis a model for the love we hope they find as they grow older.

And maybe, just maybe, we're giving them a blueprint we never had on how to stay with someone for a lifetime.

# Chapter Six

# They Said This Was Going to Be Hard

*Everybody said being a parent was hard. I knew it would be, and yet there were still so many things about being a dad that I wasn't ready for. Many things caught me off guard, seemingly coming out of nowhere, and affected me in quite a profound way. I could only deal with them as best as I could.*

## Stepping It up a Notch

If you were to grade my level of involvement as a father, I'd be pretty high up there. When our children were young, as soon as I walked in the door after work I'd herd them to the dinner table (sometimes I'd even remember to set it, too). Then I'd talk with them about their day, give them their medicines and vitamins, get them changed into their pajamas, take them to the bathroom, and put them to bed. Five nights a week. When they woke up in the middle of the night upset, I, as the Night Watchman, was the one they would call. On the weekends, I spent almost every moment I could with them, and would often have special time with them, just the three of us. Sometimes I'd even spend entire weekends with them on my own, when Gem was away. At the time, I couldn't imagine how I could have been more involved.

Well, when Gem started working full-time, I learned that there was a whole area of their lives I hadn't been involved in at all: their school.

When our kids started going to preschool, I had very little to do with it. Gem would take them every morning and pick them up every afternoon, and when I got home, I got to hear how their day went. I wasn't involved in this aspect of their lives because it wasn't necessary or really at all possible. I couldn't take them to school without showing up to work two hours late and couldn't pick them up from school without leaving work quite early. My lack of involvement in this regard meant that I didn't know what was involved in their going to school.

Then Gem started working full-time, and there were mornings when she had to leave early or nights when she came home late. I found myself needing to step up my game a notch in order to meet the new challenges in our family life.

I began making more dinners—certainly not one of my strengths. But I tried and learned. I reminded myself that the only way I would get better at it was if I did it more. I began making their lunches as well, and dealing with the notes from teachers, requests from other parents, and all of the stuff that I had no idea went on inside their backpacks every single day.

After years of building my relationship with my children and becoming increasingly comfortable as a parent, it was weird to feel not so confident again, to be uncertain all over again. While Gem handled the school routine with ease, I was stuck trying to figure out if they needed one or two snacks, or if they needed juice.

I tried to be kind to myself, to remember that every time we do something new, we're not perfect at it immediately. Plus, my not doing it perfectly was better than Gem's doing everything herself. Not to mention we were modeling new behaviors for our kids to see. They were seeing that Mommy could work outside the home and that Daddy could deal with homework and lunches and even cook (sort of). I never saw my dad do those things, and I hoped my being more involved with school and lunches would make it easier for them—especially Lucas.

And, guess what? They didn't starve. I may have forgotten the juice a time or two, and I may have produced some "interesting" dinners, but we're all okay. And I've learned that I can do more than I thought I could—a nice reminder that being a parent constantly challenges me to grow as a person.

Jeremy G. Schneider

## The Glass Is More Full Than I Thought

We have a strange problem. Books. Our okapis leave books everywhere. And I mean everywhere. The bedrooms, the floors, the office, the living room, the dining room, the kitchen table, even in the bathroom—you can find a pile of books in all these places. Heck, each car has a collection of books as well. There are even some in the bookcase.

Gem and I are constantly telling our kids to put their books away. They'll read before breakfast when they're supposed to be getting ready for school. They'll read during breakfast if we're not in the room. We had to get little reading lights for the cars so they could read when we're traveling at night. Once in a while Gem and I find ourselves so frustrated by all the books …

… before we catch ourselves. Yes, it is frustrating that they leave books all over the place. But how wonderful we've created an environment where they can read pretty much anywhere, at any time. And they love it—love to read, love to tell us what they're reading, love to share books with each other. And whenever we catch ourselves, we have one of those parenting moments when we realize that maybe we're doing okay here.

I, particularly, find it so easy to dwell on the negative (that is, sadly, my style, my genetic inheritance), to see the glass as half empty. I get frustrated when they don't listen, when they leave books all over the place even though we've told them to put them away a thousand times, instead of remembering that all those books mean our kids are reading, exactly what we had hoped for.

We started reading to our little okapis when they were still inside of Gem. We read to them almost every single night when they were little, and we almost always allow them ten to fifteen minutes of reading on their own before they go to sleep. We buy them books as presents. We buy them books when they do well at something. We buy them books as fun surprises. And they devour them. And then they switch with each other and devour some more. They've probably read most of their books twice, and the good ones more than that.

The fact that books are all over our house, in places we don't want them, isn't really a bad thing. It's a sign that we have succeeded in at least one area of parenting.

From that perspective, the glass looks pretty full.

### "But I Don't Want to Be Bigger!"

One night we all went out for Chinese food. Preparing my son for the frigid cold, I started zipping up his jacket but had a little bit trouble. I turned to my wife and said, "I think we need to get him another jacket. He's getting too big for this one."

"No!" he almost screamed.

"What, Lucas?"

"No, but I'm not getting big. I don't want to be bigger!"

I'd always thought that most children wanted to grow up fast. Being older or bigger means having privileges, rights. It means being able to do things you aren't able to do when you're younger. It's only as we get older that we wish for time to slow down, to pass less rapidly. So I found myself perplexed when I learned that neither of my three-year-olds really wanted the privileges of growing up.

My children started sleeping in toddler beds when they were a little older than two and a half. We transitioned them after they made some serious attempts to climb out of their cribs (Lucas even jumped out in anger once) and complained that they didn't want to sleep in them anymore. But about six months later, they began telling me, several times a week, that they wanted their cribs back, that they missed their cribs. While Gem and I were pretty certain that if we brought the cribs back into their room they would get very upset, we didn't want to find out. There would be no going back.

In addition, my children had absolutely no desire to use a potty. None whatsoever. I joked that they would see the benefits when they were packing to go off to college, that when they had to choose between a suitcase of clothes and iPod accessories and that silly box of diapers, they would finally say, "Oh, I don't need those anymore." Then, and only then, would we finally be done with diapers. We tried so many things to persuade, bribe, entice, but they were adamant. Sure, they complained when we changed their diapers, but even that didn't make them want to use the potty.

That summer, Lucas and Dorit would be starting camp, and in the fall they would be going to preschool for the first time. But we couldn't use school as an incentive for potty training because our twins didn't want to go to school either. They had never been to daycare because we didn't want anyone else taking care of them. Now, they didn't want to leave Mommy; they didn't want to go to school.

My children didn't want to be bigger, they didn't want to grow up, they didn't want to lose the special status of being babies. This "phase" seemed to drag on for a rather long time. They were fearful of the unknown future and the changes it might bring. They wanted the comfort of what was familiar, of Mommy, and hopefully, even of Daddy. When I thought about it that way, I could understand that.

I wondered, were Gem and I somehow sending them the message that we didn't want them to grow up? Or maybe we were pushing them too hard to grow up? I really didn't think so, though I wasn't certain enough to rule it out. I did know we were dealing with a force we didn't fully understand—the toddler mind.

One of the reasons I became a therapist was because I've always been able to understand people, their motives, their thought processes; to intuit their feelings. This has certainly helped me with my children— more than I ever imagined, actually. But the lack of communication in this situation was like a gulf between us and them. They couldn't tell us what was going on. They probably didn't even know. But it was and is our job to help them, regardless, without hurting them too badly in the process.

It was a case of growing pains for us all. Gem and I were stuck in the middle of two opposing forces: my children on one side, wanting to stay exactly the way they were, not wanting to get older and face the reality of school and bigger clothes and everything else that signals getting older. Reality on the other. My kids were getting bigger, outgrowing their clothes, harder to pick up and approaching that time when they spend more time at school than at home. What made it even more difficult was that while I was tired of changing diapers and cleaning up after their messy eating, I was sad to see their clothes getting too small for them. I was sad to see the toddler accent disappear. I was sad that my little girl was no longer easily fitting on my chest and that carrying them both at the same time was getting harder and harder.

Their first years were the best years I'd ever had, and a part of me didn't want anything to change. But I tried to keep my own bittersweet tug-of-war buried in a corner of my heart, hoping that they wouldn't notice, hoping that their growing-up experience would continue to be the most incredible time of my life.

## Pee and Poop—There, I've Said It!

I've written many articles about fatherhood, but for a long time I avoided one particular subject, even though it was a major part of our lives. The main reason was that I was uncomfortable with the whole discussion. I handled helping our three-year-olds learn to use the potty better than I thought I would—especially considering the issues and major levels of discomfort I experienced—but that didn't mean I liked talking about it.

In my family, no one ever "went to the bathroom." In fact, I thought that if people knew I went to the bathroom (as if they didn't), they would see me as less of a person. I thought that going to the bathroom was a weakness, a flaw in my being (as if the whole world doesn't do it every single day, too). I've worked hard to become comfortable going to the bathroom and trying not to care whether other people know. But talking about it with other people, well, that's a whole other issue.

If it weren't for Gem, I would probably have made essentially no progress on this issue. Ironically (or maybe fortunately), I married a sexuality educator, and she has no issues about this stuff whatsoever. In fact, she has the opposite of issues. She has strengths and skills that she's (unknowingly) teaching me. Of course, there's also something about changing diapers every day that's like trial by fire—you either get used to dealing with poop and pee or you crack under the pressure and run screaming down the street completely naked with diapers in your hands. In the early days, we were changing diapers every three hours or so (yes, that was about twelve to fourteen diaper changes a day). The only way to stop changing diapers was to stop feeding them and, as you can imagine, we didn't think that was a good approach to the problem.

Of course, as our children got older, I was constantly challenged to grow as well. Once I got used to changing diapers and talking about poop, then we had to talk about what *kinds* of poops they were having. And how many times a day they were happening. Then we started helping our kids understand that we don't use diapers, we use the … toilet. Ugh, I still hate the terminology of all this. Really. I was cringing as I wrote this, my fingers afraid to touch the keyboard after writing the offending words.

The women in our family, my children's mother, their tita, their nana, and their abuelita—all would let our children into the bathroom with them to show them how people use a toilet. It took me a long time to be able to do that. Like months and months, not weeks. I'd spent my life never letting anyone know I actually went to the bathroom; to let someone (really, two someones) come with me and watch was so far beyond my comfort level that it made me anxious just thinking about it.

As with many of these situations where I needed to be better at something as a parent, what helped me was the idea that my role as father was more important than anything I felt as a person. My children needed to see their father go to the bathroom, too, to understand that both men and women use the bathroom and that men use it differently than women. Who else was going to show that to my son if not me? I had to rise to that challenge even if it made me terribly uncomfortable because it wasn't about me, it was about them.

Interestingly, despite our best efforts, our children steadfastly refused to participate in toilet education. They didn't really mind diapers (though they hated having them changed—if it had been up to them, they would have just worn one diaper all day regardless of whether it was wet or dry, empty or full). And they didn't have much interest in being like Gem and me. We tried so many different techniques, including flat-out bribery. Finally, Gem and I concocted a new plan (in case you haven't noticed, parenting is so much about problem solving; it's one of the things I really enjoy about it). We would let Lucas off the hook, since he often didn't respond well to pressure, and focus instead on Dorit, since she liked the limelight, challenges, and rewards. This approach worked, and once Dorit got it, Lucas came along shortly thereafter.

Once Dorit was using the potty, I found myself sitting next to my little girl while she peed and/or pooped, encouraging her, congratulating her, helping her to clean herself, and even cleaning out the potty (more cringing) after she was done. How had this happened? What had I become?

I had become a man who understands that to be the kind of father I wanted to be, I needed to be more than I was; I needed to be what they needed me to be. I didn't want to infect them with my issues on the subject—that was critical. I didn't want them cringing or feeling uncomfortable about something completely normal. My children needed their father to show them how to use the toilet. They needed both of their parents to show them that using the bathroom and saying "pee" and "poop" and, yes, "toilet," was okay. They're just words like any other.

What's amazing is that the more I said them, the more that became true for me, too.

## Sometimes School Can Be Hard

One night when our children were three and a half years old, Gem and I were getting them ready for bed and it was time for Lucas to sit on the potty (which was in our living room so the other could use the bathroom).

"Read me a book, Daddy?"

"We don't have time for a book, but how about we talk about what you did at school today?"

"Okay!" He was so excited that he backed into the couch when he meant to sit down on the potty. We both laughed.

I started asking him what he did at school, and if he'd gone to the gym.

"Yeah," he replied.

"What did you do?"

"Played Ring Around the Rosie."

"Yeah? Did you like it?"

"No, we played Duck, Duck, Goose!"

"Oh, where you run around the circle?"

"Yeah," he said with a big smile.

"What else did you do at the gym?"

"Melodee cried."

"Melodee was crying in the gym?"

"Yeah."

"Did you go over to her?"

"No, but we played with her and she stopped crying." What does "go over to her" mean, anyway? I loved that he answered my questions, despite how clumsily I asked them.

"You and Dorit played with her?"

"Yeah."

"That was very sweet of you, Lucas." He smiled. "Do you know why she was crying?"

"No, she just cried."

"Sometimes school can be hard, huh?"

"Yeah."

And BAM! Then came the flashbacks—memories of sitting in school by myself, knowing I had no one at home for me, no one at school. I was dealing with not only the normal difficulties of childhood alone, but additional family trauma as well. The place I felt safe was by myself, at school, even though that time only made me feel lonelier.

I looked at my beautiful, sensitive, intelligent little boy while he was sitting on the potty (how many intimate moments have I had with my children while they were on the potty?) and felt overwhelmed by how in love with him I was, by how much this little being meant to me, by how much I desperately wanted to prevent him from feeling that kind of pain and loneliness.

I reached my hand out to gently caress his face, afraid that if I did anything else I might overwhelm him with everything I was feeling.

" You know I love you, right? I love you very much, Lucas."

" I know," he said, smiling at Silly Daddy. "I love you, too, Daddy."

With all the strength I could muster, I continued the conversation. "So, did you get to walk around going Duck ... Duck ... Goose?"

He giggled. "Yeah."

I might not be able to prevent him from feeling any pain, but I hoped that this relationship he and I were building together, these special moments we were sharing, would help ensure that he never felt painfully alone, as I did.

## Sounds of Torture

In the war on their parents, in the battle for sanity in the okapi household, our children had taken their attack to the next level. Just as the United States military uses certain kinds of music to wear down the enemy, or even specific songs to torture detainees, to break their will, our twins used sounds to achieve similar goals with us. Except they used their own voices.

Lucas started this screaming—screeching, really—at the top of his lungs whenever something didn't go quite his way. Actually, even if he just thought it wasn't going his way he would begin to scream and screech.

I came home every night around the same time, and when I came home we would have dinner together. One night, when I told Lucas it was time to go downstairs for dinner, he said, "No!"

No?

I repeated myself. Then he started getting upset about wanting to play some more, really getting himself worked up. So Dorit and I went downstairs and left him up there. Then he started really screeching because no one was paying him any attention. Finally, Gem and I said if he continued screeching, he would get a time-out. He stopped. Barely.

But while I ABSOLUTELY hated the screeching, at least I understood that Lucas was doing it because he was angry and trying to express himself. Dorit's loon imitation was what pushed my wife and me over the edge.

When our twins were babies, I had bought them toy birds. If you pressed them, they made the sounds of their real-world counterparts. At the time, I thought they were pretty cool—I love birds and I loved that the toys really did sound like the real things. (Honestly, I still like them and would get more if I thought Gem would still live with me.) The loon, however, makes kind of a disturbing sound, and at one point, Gem asked me to take it to the office so she wouldn't have to hear it anymore.

I guess one of the times our children came to my office, they saw the loon and took it back home with them. And Dorit mastered the loon call. If she were to go out into the marshlands, I bet she'd be able to attract an entire loon colony (do you think there's any money to be made from this "gift?"). At first, I didn't care so much, but it was pushing my beloved right to the edge. She has the most sensitive hearing of anyone I've ever known, especially when it comes to sounds she doesn't want to hear. The loon call quickly became one of the most offensive sounds she could possibly experience.

The first thing we tried to do was ignore her. We tried for almost two weeks, I think. She didn't care—she only did it more. So then we started counting as soon as Dorit began making the call, trying to get her to stop (if we got to three, she got a time-out on the stairs). Somewhere in that process, her loon call came to symbolize how she JUST DIDN'T GIVE A CRAP WHAT WE SAID! While the noise itself didn't really upset me, when I heard it coming out of her mouth I would become furious because she knew we didn't want her to make that sound, and she just didn't care. She was unfazed by us. We were powerless to stop her.

And just when we were at our wits' end, she stopped.

I'm certain we did nothing to make it stop. She probably became bored with it. Over the years, they (particularly Dorit) hit on other sounds, words, and actions they knew made us insane, and while at the time we weren't sure how we would survive, we continued to do so somehow. So much of our kids' lives were controlled by us, and I've got to believe there was a real sense of joy and even power in being a little child able to make big Mommy and Daddy a little crazy.

While I get that, I still think it would have behooved us to invest in earplugs.

## Terrible Twos? How about the Tortuous Threes?

Everyone warned us about the Terrible Twos. I say, Terrible Twos? Pshaw! How about the Tortuous Threes?

When Dorit was about three and a half years old, her behavior took a significant turn for the worse. My precious little girl had never been an easy child. But while her bad moments were bad, her good moments had been quite amazing. Until she hit the Tortuous Threes, when she began "saving" all of her bad moments for us and sharing all of her good ones with others. It felt deliberate, almost. As if she wanted people to think of us as pathetic parents for saying how exhausted and drained we were.

Dorit could go from zero to a hundred and sixty in two seconds. Everything would be fine and then BAM! She'd be screaming, throwing her head back, or dropping to the floor: "BUT I WANTED TO DO THAT!" You'd think we were saying no to a request to continue breathing instead of a request to wear a dress on a cold, rainy day. Sometimes the outburst would be one mini-explosion and then she'd calm down. But often it would last for several minutes or even longer.

Almost every single thing became a battle with her: going to the potty, getting dressed, being buckled into her car seat, sitting at the table, eating, and being quiet and not waking up Lucas in the morning. She was in time-out about three times a day. She didn't care. She knew she could take us when push came to shove. We were older and more tired. She had youth, energy, and exuberance. We didn't have a chance.

When our twins were babies, it was clear that there was no "malicious" intent when they screamed and cried; they were just babies. When they became toddlers, we began teaching them what was right and wrong, what was okay and not okay, how to behave properly and how not to behave, but we knew they wouldn't get it right away. We were still getting to know them, beginning to see their personalities develop and starting to see real signs of intelligence.

But by this point they were preschoolers. I felt as if I could really see their potential, what they were capable of. So when they behaved badly or did something they knew they shouldn't be doing, I found it much harder to handle. As preschoolers, it seemed they were choosing to misbehave, to intentionally ignore what we'd said, to break the rules. And, of course, they were.

(Isn't it nice to see that even a father with a master's degree in marriage and family therapy can be just as befuddled and frustrated as anyone else by the behaviors that accompany each developmental stage? You're welcome.)

One morning we were having bagels for breakfast and Dorit started using her finger to clean the top of the bagel container. Since that had gone well for her, she started licking the container top.

"Did Daddy say that was okay?" Gem asked her.

"Daddy, can I lick the top?"

"No, Dorit," I said, and walked into the kitchen to toast my bagel. You'll never guess who was licking the top of the container when I returned. I'll give you a hint. It wasn't Lucas, or Gem, or their Uncle H or his girlfriend.

That's a time-out in my book.

Of course, that was her third of the day already, and it was only 10:30 a.m.

As mentioned, what made it even more frustrating was that she would behave so well with everyone else. So when we tried to talk to the grandparents about it, they didn't really understand. (And, of course, because they're grandparents, they don't have to worry about minor details like limits and consequences. I can't wait for that perk, I gotta tell ya.)

One night Dorit refused to open her mouth when it was time to brush her teeth. Finally she did but then clamped it shut on the toothbrush so I couldn't actually move it around in her mouth. She knew that this frustrated me, and she smiled until I told her I was going to start counting and that at three, she would get a time-out and then have to come right back to the bathroom to start over until we got her teeth brushed.

A variation of *1-2-3 Magic* written by Thomas W. Phelan had worked very well in the past. If she (or Lucas) behaved badly once, she would get a One and be told that at Three she would get a time-out. If she did it again, she would get a Two. One more time and she would go directly to time-out (do not pass Go, do not collect two hundred dollars). For some reason, when I used the One, Two, Three Magic system, I almost never raised my voice or got upset. It helped me stay calm and in control.

A good example of how it helped me to not lose my temper even while I might have been losing my mind.

"Dorit."

Nothing. She was five feet away.

"Dorit," I said, a little more loudly, just in case she hadn't actually heard me.

Nothing.

So, in a softer voice: "That's one."

Head snapped around. SHE'D HEARD ME. Sometimes, to really mess with me, she would wait for the count of two before being all like, "What? What? Did you say something, Daddy?"

Made. Me. In. Sane.

Her choosing to not listen to me was one of the hardest things to deal with. It felt personal. I know that by making it personal, by taking it personally, I only made the situation worse. But damn was it hard to re-member that in the moment.

On the one hand, I'm so glad I have a strong-willed daughter. She's smart, tough, and assertive—the way I want her to be. I just didn't know about the side effects, so to speak. I didn't want to stomp out her strong sense of identity, but I didn't want to fight with her over everything or, heaven forbid, give her the notion that she was running things in the okapi household, because that would have been the end of our existence, I'm sure. (Or was I deluded for believing she didn't already have this notion?)

If I could figure out how to consistently apply One, Two, Three instead of getting upset (and edging too close to that insanity line), and then fig-ure out how to effectively ignore their bad behavior instead of getting upset, I figured I'd be in pretty good shape.

I might master it by the time they're off to college.

## What about Their Impact on Me?

I was just doing the calculations in my head: today is somewhere around the 2,582nd time I've had to leave my family to go to work. Today is also Monday, and Mondays are always worse than other days because I spend all weekend with my family. First days back after long weekends are even worse, and first days back after vacations are the worst of all.

But today …

Today is a new kind of bad. It ranks up there as one of the absolute worst.

Today is not only Monday—it's also the day after a long weekend with my family. But the real kicker is that today is the first day in almost a week that I'm not home with my kids taking care of them. Gem went on a business trip last week, and I was a "single" dad to my almost-nine-year-old twins for a few days.

I loved it!

It was the first time I'd had a few days being the only parent since they started school. Before, I'd only been a "single" dad on the weekends or during days off. I got them up and showered in the morning, made their breakfasts and lunches, drove them to school, picked them up, helped them with their homework, got them ready for their after-school activities, dealt with their worries and fears, made dinners, and got them to bed without any real problems—though there were some awfully intense highs and lows. My little girl had a tough time with her mother's being away, and demonstrated just how poorly she could behave the first night. It was pretty terrible and there was no one to turn to, but we got through it.

Normally, I miss out on most of this. I particularly liked picking them up from school and hearing all about it while it was still fresh in their minds. I liked seeing their teachers and watching them interact with their friends. I also liked taking them to their music lessons and Hebrew school. I got a real feel for where my kids go and whom they interact with—normally I only hear about these things.

I've missed out on so much by working, and I wish it didn't have to be that way.

But the experience also made me realize something. I've done quite a bit of research on the impact involved dads have on kids (improved self-esteem, fewer behavioral problems, better school experiences, higher levels of satisfaction as adults, etc.), but what about the impact of kids on their dads?

Even though I go to work, I'm an involved dad, and this involvement has made me a better man, has helped me to understand my priorities more clearly than ever before, has awakened something inside of me I never knew existed. I love my children and I love being with them, love being there for them. Yes, I certainly hope my involvement in their lives will make a big difference for them, but it's obvious that it has already made a significant difference in mine.

I'm going to miss them something awful today.

## The Wisdom of the Band-Aid Theory

At four years old, Lucas refused to go to sleep at night. He would scream instead. I was extremely frustrated, and felt certain that the issues he was having with going to school and going to sleep boiled down to the same thing—separation. I'd been intensely trying to help him go to sleep smoothly at night for eight months by that point, and I was running out of patience. And because I was upset about leaving him at school (I didn't want him to feel as if we were abandoning him, as if we didn't love him), I was unwilling to let him cry it out (okay, Gem also didn't want that to happen). But it didn't matter what I did or said—he insisted on making the process as difficult as possible.

I tried everything I could think of to keep him from crying it out, and I always failed. Always. Every single time he got upset, I went upstairs to try to calm him down, get him into bed, and help him think about all of his happy thoughts so that he could go to sleep. For the most part it only reinforced for him that if he got upset, he would get to spend more time with me. That was clearly not my goal.

This went on for several weeks until one night, out of utter frustration, when he started screaming and banging on the door, I picked him up and put him back into bed without saying a word. I think the shock of my not saying anything stunned him enough that he simply went back to sleep. But the next night, it didn't work the first time I tried it. I had to do it four or five times that night, and again the following night five or six times. Lucas's screaming was getting Dorit upset as well.

The night after that, he started his screaming and banging about ten seconds after I closed his door, and he did the same after I put him back into his bed. So I gritted my teeth, put him back into bed once more, and told him that I wasn't coming back up for the rest of the night. He cried and screamed as I left. And I let him. I refused to go up anymore.

After about five minutes, he was quiet and presumably asleep. Is it any wonder parents feel as if their kids are smarter than they are?

I'd been thinking a lot about how to help him adjust smoothly to going to sleep and school without causing the pain I'd vowed never to inflict on him. But I had to wonder if I'd been only dragging out the torture. Going up to his room and trying to calm him down would momentarily stop the crying, maybe even hold off the pain, but when I left again, it was like reopening a wound—the pain would pick up where it had left off. If there was one thing I had learned from leaving him in the morning every single weekday, it was that leaving had to be like removing a Band-Aid. If you do it slowly, the pain drags on. If you rip it off quickly, there's a moment of fierce pain, but then everything is okay.

Clearly, I'd needed to apply that wisdom earlier when it came to the other area where separation was an issue for my boy—going to sleep.

**They Don't Need Sports Like I Did**

Sports helped save my life. My childhood was not a good one. I was miserable and depressed and didn't have any self-confidence whatsoever because of it—except when I was on the field or the court. When I was playing sports, it seemed I was a different person, someone who had skills and talents and could do almost anything. Seriously. My college entrance essay was about how I helped our team win the soccer championship—even though I was terribly sick.

I was never good at school; my favorite class was gym. But I always looked forward to the summer. For six years, I attended an all-sports summer day camp and then on the weekends I played baseball all day with my neighborhood friends. I learned not only how to play many different types of sports, but that I was pretty good at them: good enough to even set some camp records, which seemed like a huge deal at the time. Sports achievements were the only accomplishments I had, the only things that made me feel good, the only things that made me feel happy.

But in college, I met a woman and fell in love—even though she didn't like sports at all. I would watch my favorite teams play (I was born in Philly and still love the Phillies, Eagles, Flyers, Sixers) when I could, but I also started excelling in my classes. A new kind of confidence grew.

Before long Gem and I got married (no sports-themed wedding for us), and then we had our twins. I've tried to get them into sports, but it's just not there, they don't feel it. And I've found myself torn. Sports were so important to me as a kid, an incredible resource, and I want my kids to have this resource as well. But I don't want to push them into something they don't care about. They don't really like watching sports with me, don't really understand the games, and just aren't that interested.

On one level it's sad, because it's a part of me I'm not able to share with them. But on the other hand, I'm relieved. I needed sports because everything else in my life was so terrible. Sport was the only good thing I had, and I used it as much as I could.

My children, however, don't need sports like I did. Sure, it would be nice if they knew how to play and watch (and I suspect they will at some point—even if just to humor me). But my kids are smart, so much smarter than I was at their age. They are voracious readers and LOVE school. I hated school. They're almost sad when they have a day off.

And they are loved like no other children I've ever known. They don't need sports to make them feel good about themselves. They have Gem and me and grandparents and aunts and uncles; and now great teachers and friends. They have more than I ever dreamed of when I was their age.

I do hope they get into sports a little bit, for the health benefits and the sense of team, but I won't push them. They already have what they need, and I am incredibly grateful for that.

**Remembering to Smell the Roses**

It's easy to get so wrapped up in a goal that we forget to enjoy the process.

When Dorit was nearly five years old, she decided she didn't want to wear diapers at night anymore. Gem and I had been encouraging our twins to sleep diaper-free for several months. First, we decreased the amount of water in the sippy cups they kept on their night tables. Then we stopped leaving water for them at night altogether. We also tried to encourage them to get up and come to our room for help when they needed to go to the bathroom. Unfortunately, that didn't work out so well. Changing two sets of sheets at three thirty in the morning wasn't a fun way to start the day—for any of us.

But Dorit refused to give up. Much like her Daddy, I'm proud to say, once my little girl makes up her mind, she commits to achieving her goal. She decided she only wanted to wear underpants at night, and she would do whatever it took to make that happen.

And so would I.

After talking to our pediatrician, Gem and I decided we would wake her up before we went to bed and take her to the bathroom. I took that responsibility on, waking her up around eleven each night to take her to the bathroom.

I didn't think this chore would be fun. Would she want to be woken up? Would this just be another fight? Would we wake up her brother, sleeping in the other bed in their room? Would it affect her sleep? Would she be able to fall asleep again afterwards? Would she want me to stay with her? If Dorit didn't get enough sleep, we'd all suffer.

The first night, I gently woke her up.

"Dorit. Come on. Let's go to the bathroom."

She popped out of bed. "Okay, Daddy." She was ready. We held hands walking down the hall to the bathroom and held hands on the way back. She crawled into bed and fell fast asleep before I was even out the door.

The second night she was more tired, but did very well. More hand holding, and I even got an "I love you" as I walked out of their room.

By the third night, she was so tired that I had to pick her up out of bed. When my little girl molds her body to mine when she's tired, I experience one of the best feelings I've had as a father. She wraps her arms and legs around my body, puts her head on my shoulder, and melts into me. It's a feeling of closeness like no other. It was so wonderful that night that I barely even felt her weight as I carried her down the hall. If someone had told me that being a daddy felt like this, I wouldn't have been so scared about becoming one.

She went to the bathroom and afterwards, I offered to carry her back. She didn't say anything, but after she dried her hands, she reached up to me. I gladly picked her up and carried her back to her bed.

"I love you, Sweetie Girl."

"I love you, too, Daddy." And she fell asleep.

I'd thought the process was going to be such a hassle, another thing for me to remember before I could go to bed at night. Instead, not only was I helping my little girl achieve something she really wanted, but I also got one more cuddle, one more special moment with her.

And there can never be too many of those.

**Don't Worry about Movie Time until It's Movie Time**

It's amazing how some things click with my okapis and some don't. Sometimes—especially when they're upset—I feel as if I'm throwing anything I can think of to try to help them, hoping something sticks, something helps them feel better or understand what's happening. Sometimes I have these great ideas and my okapis don't even bat an eye when I share them. And sometimes, a spur-of-the-moment thought changes everything.

Gem and I sent our kids to camp one summer, and for some frustrating reason, every afternoon the camp would show a movie (why they would show a movie in the afternoon during the summer boggles the mind). Before long, every night Dorit would start worrying about the movie.

"It's dark, Daddy. And there are so many people."

Gem and I tried everything to help her feel better. We let her take a stuffed animal. We let her take a small flashlight. We let her take a notebook and some crayons. We talked to the camp. These things helped a little, but not enough.

Soon she was having trouble going to sleep at night because she was so worried about movie time, which didn't even start until 4:00 p.m. the following day. When she wasn't worried, she would say that she had enjoyed the day, but her anxiety about movie time was taking over, ruining her enjoyment. And it was ruining her nights as well. She was sleeping less, which in turn made her more sensitive and more anxious, more easily upset. Gem and I were becoming increasingly frustrated and desperate.

"I'm worried about movie time, Daddy," she said to me one night from the bed in her loft.

"Sweetie Girl, you're worrying so much about something that isn't happening for a long time," I said, standing on the ladder of her bunk bed looking into her face.

"But it's tomorrow, Daddy."

"Yes, but tomorrow afternoon. You have a whole day of fun before movie time even happens."

And then it hit me.

"What if you could schedule your worry, Sweetie Girl? I'm not asking you not to worry. I'm saying let's not worry until you have movie time. That way, you can enjoy your day."

"Can I do that?" she asked innocently, as if I could really decide how the world works.

"Sure," I said, realizing this could be it—the solution. "Don't worry about movie time until it's movie time."

I can't tell you this changed her life and she had a great time at camp, but it definitely helped. She started sleeping better, which gave her more energy to deal with her day, making movie time more bearable. She never enjoyed it, but it became much less of a stressor.

More importantly, this became a saying in our family. Anytime someone starts worrying about something too far in advance, someone else will say, "Don't worry about movie time until it's movie time." In fact, my wife and I even say it to each other when we're worried about something at work. Not only does it make sense, but it evokes rich memories of how it helped all of us before.

It's also a nice reminder that parenting is a lot like playing a sport—soccer, for instance. If you just keep kicking the ball on goal, at some point you're going to score. And then it won't matter that you missed all of those other shots. All that matters is that you scored one goal, that you helped your child when she needed you.

We don't necessarily know which shot will go in the net, but if we keep trying, one of them will.

# Chapter Seven

# They're Not Little Anymore!

*Before I was a dad, I never imagined the range of emotions and challenges I'd be faced with as my okapis grew older and bigger. I'd only thought about babies and toddlers, not about tweens and teens. But those years come, and they bring with them new challenges—and opportunities.*

### More Than a Double Stroller

The okapis' double stroller is sitting in the basement taking up valuable space, but I just don't know what to do with it. Somehow shoving it in the garage doesn't seem a just ending for this device that has been with us for so many years. It used to live in our Subaru Outback, and was always there when we needed it. It's been to Pennsylvania, Rhode Island, New Jersey, Florida, and even Ecuador with us, not to mention the mall, the park—hundreds of places.

I remember shopping for double strollers, still shocked that we were having two kids instead of one. My wife was already on bed rest at the time. It was one of the only purchases we made for the okapis where I felt I'd contributed something. I tested a couple of different kinds in the store, trying to figure out which one would be best for our soon-to-be-born children.

I remember the pride I felt pushing the stroller through Manhattan; everyone would stop to admire our cute little twins. "Yup," I'd say, beaming. "I'm their Daddy." Those first few months were so difficult, but when I was pushing my babies in the stroller, I really felt like a father, like these two little beings were mine.

I remember when we moved out of NYC and I put the stroller in the back of our car. There it sat, day in and day out for over a year, always there when we needed it. Sometimes we had to pile food on top of it after a visit to Costco.

I remember realizing our okapis had learned to unbuckle the straps, that they could stand up and put their feet on the wheels and stop our forward momentum, forcing the handlebars into the gut of whoever was pushing the stroller.

I remember asking my wife, once the okapis started walking, "Should we bring the stroller?" She often wanted to, but I felt it was cumbersome, a burden. "Let's let our children run free, now that they can," I'd say.

Then one day, one of us took the stroller out of the car and it was never put back. There was nothing special about that day. I have no idea when it happened. I know on every single trip we've taken since, neither one of us has said, "Oh man, I wish we had the stroller." No, the stroller's glory days are over, and it sits in our basement like an old racehorse put out to pasture with nothing to do, no purpose to serve.

The problem is, I can't move it. If I move it, I'll be forced to admit why we don't need it any longer. I'll be forced to admit Lucas and Dorit are no longer babies, that they're growing up.

I'll move that stroller when I'm ready.

## Loving Him at School

I had the privilege of taking my kids to third grade the other day. It's funny because I do it enough that I know what to do, but not enough that I've gotten good at it. It takes me fifteen minutes to get their lunches ready. My wife can do it in less than five. And I worry so much about getting them to school on time because I can never remember how long each "step" takes. Getting dressed is how long? Eating breakfast? Brushing teeth and hair?

But the walk there is usually quite nice because I know how long that takes, and it always feels like special time, Los Tres Amigos together. Often one or both of them will hold my hand. When it's cold we do this thing we started at the zoo a couple of years ago—a perfect example of how something so seemingly meaningless can have such weight in their lives. It was very cold that day, and my kids' hands were cold. I'm a short guy, and the sleeves of my jackets are always a bit too long. I told my kids to put their hands in my sleeves so we could hold hands and they wouldn't be too cold. Now every time it's cold out and we're walking together, they ask if they can do it again.

When we got to school, they each gave me a hug and a kiss, and I told them I loved them. I watched them run into the school with their friends.

But then Lucas turned around and said, "I love you, Daddy."

He has this unbelievably sweet way about him. I look at him in these moments and wonder if this was what I was like as a kid, a sensitive boy who genuinely cared about others, before I was hurt in so many ways. I'd like to think he's a better version, a purer version of me, that he has taken the good parts of me and combined them with an intelligence and creativity that I didn't have until I was an adult. There is something quite amazing about seeing ourselves in our children. I feel hopeful when I think of all that lies ahead of him, but also some sadness when I think of what he has that I didn't.

"I love you, too," I replied, and immediately wondered how much longer he'd be okay with my telling him I loved him outside the school, with his friends around. It's so different for boys than girls in our society. I wondered if my daughter would always feel more comfortable receiving my love and affection in public. Being a daddy's girl is just fine, but is it okay to be a daddy's boy? It's certainly something we're going to find out.

For the time being, however, as long he lets me do it, I'm happy to do so.

## They Need Me Differently Now

One night we came home from the city late in the evening. Our kids were exhausted. For some reason, my son never wants to sleep in the car, can't seem to let himself slip into slumber. But my daughter can fall asleep anywhere, at any time. That night, she snored most of the way home.

When we arrived home, I went to help Dorit out of the car, but she woke up and walked to the house on her own.

And my heart sank a little bit.

I love my children and I love being a daddy. I love my family and the life Gem and I have built together. My family is far and away the most amazing thing that has ever happened to me. I can't imagine who I would be if I weren't part of this experience.

But my children are ten years old, and they need me differently now. After car trips, I used to hurry out of the vehicle to get Dorit so I could be the one to carry her into the house, to carry her into her bedroom. I wanted to be that daddy and it felt good, being there for her in that way.

A few days later, we were once again out a little late and Dorit was exhausted—so exhausted she didn't even want to leave. I told her that when we got home, I would carry her into the house if she wanted (do you see what a selfless daddy I am?). She nodded her sleepy head and we got into the car.

When we got home, I helped her out of the seat belt, vowing to savor every moment. As I lifted her up, I remembered that my little girl is ten years old and I might need to work out more. I can remember holding both of my kids on my chest at the same time. There was no way I was going to be able to carry my Sweetie Girl upstairs—unless I threw her over my shoulder like a sack of potatoes. I felt heavy, as though I had lost something I could never get back.

But when I put her down, she didn't look disappointed. She didn't look at me as if I'd let her down. She looked at me as though I'm her daddy, and always will be.

She might no longer need me to carry her, but she still needs me and I still need her. It's different now, but still pretty darn wonderful.

## An Answer for Bullying

When I was in college, I took a parenting course because I was terrified of being a parent (suspected I might never become one, actually). One of the things I wanted to know was what to do when my children came home from school complaining of being bullied. I wanted the answer to make everything better for them, to help them through this challenge. When I was a kid, I was bullied and no one seemed to care; I had to learn to deal with it all by myself (I was fast, so I ran away). Today, there are dozens and dozens of articles about bullying in all its forms. Apparently, I wasn't the only one who wanted to know about this.

But now that I'm actually a parent, the issue seems less worrisome than it did. Sure, I don't want my kids to get bullied. But if they do, they can come to me and their mother to talk about it. That's big. It's bad enough to be bullied, but being bullied with no one to turn to is even more painful.

And I know what I want them to know. I want my okapis to know they are loved, immensely and unconditionally. I want them to know that bullies don't know what they're talking about, that they're trying to make themselves feel better by making others feel worse. I want them to know that these bullies probably don't have the family we do, that those kids aren't in a loving family like we are, that they are probably pretty sad and angry, though this is no excuse.

I want them to think about whether they can talk to a teacher about what the bully is doing, or if they can talk to their friends to work together against the bully. I don't want them to forget that they have people they can turn to in school if that's where it's happening.

I also want them to learn to defend themselves, to stand up for themselves. This is a skill they'll need for the rest of their lives. Bullies aren't just in school, but in the workplace as well, and we all need help dealing with people like this. If we can teach our children this skill now, think how much easier it will be for them as they grow up and deal with others like this.

I know Gem and I can help them practice, help them work out things to say so they get comfortable standing up for themselves. I'm also one of the more sarcastic people on the planet; my kids have been absorbing sarcasm for years, and their practice standing up to me with quick thinking and quick reactions can only help as well.

But I'm not afraid to let them fight for themselves. If words don't work, if these bullies actually physically hurt them, and the school isn't holding up its part, my kids have my permission to kick ass. Maybe that's not what the school wants me to say, but if the teachers aren't around, if our kids try to use words, try to walk away, try to stand up for themselves and these bullies go too far, Gem and I will defend them without hesitation. Unfortunately, sometimes bullies need to find out the hard way that others aren't an easy target.

Fighting back physically is by no means the best solution, but it is an option available to them. To me, that's the key; my kids need to know they have options when dealing with bullies, and that they can talk to their teachers, to their friends, to us. They need to know we'll help them practice facing these bullies, that they'll never have to deal with something like this all alone. When I took that parenting class oh so many years ago, this was what I wanted to learn.

Our kids are off to a better start than I was, that's for sure.

## Is This Really the Best It Can Be?

Gem and I were trying to catch up with each other after a long day. After she was done work, she'd taken our kids, eight years old at the time, to get some clothes for the Spring (even though it snowed that morning) Concert.

"Dorit had so much fun trying on clothes," she told me. Our little girl really does enjoy being "on stage," whatever the stage happens to be.

"Imagine what it will be like in a few years," I responded, thinking of my wife and teenage daughter going clothes shopping together, cleaning out the store.

"No, this is the best it's going to be."

"What do you mean?" I asked in shock.

"She's not looking at her body right now," Gem said. "She's not staring at the things she doesn't like about herself, at any imperfections she might see. She's just enjoying playing dress-up."

"Oh God …" And I felt such sadness. My little girl is, well, I don't know how to explain it.

She's not perfect. In fact, sometimes she makes me insane, seriously out-of-my-mind crazy, the way she can so easily ignore me or blatantly lie (or, as my wife likes to say, "reframe the truth") right to my face.

But God I love that girl with every fiber of my being. I love the way her smile, just like her mother's, lights up her face. I love how witty and smart she is, and how she's the most emotionally intelligent girl I've ever met. I love how much fun she can be and the look she gets when she's focused on and committed to doing something she's never done before.

And while it terrifies me, I love the way she looks at me as if all the love in the world begins in my face. I am her first love, and I take that honor quite seriously.

I tell her everyday how beautiful she is and how much I love her. And I don't just tell her when she's dressed up. I tell her when she's in her PJs, too. I hug and kiss her and tell her I love her every day before I leave for work, when I return home, and when she goes to bed (I do the same for my boy, promise).

In fact, I've read the research that shows that girls with involved fathers, girls who feel their fathers are invested in their relationship, can actually begin menstruating later, start having sex later, and are at a lower risk for teen pregnancy. Girls with involved fathers are also less likely to have eating disorders and have low self-esteem, and are more likely to be happier as adults.

I ask my little girl frequently if she knows how much I love her because the research is clear; she has to feel my love, my commitment to her, for these benefits to come into play. If she doesn't know how I feel, what I feel doesn't matter very much.

But maybe I've been deluding myself, thinking I could somehow single-handedly stop what happens to so many young girls in America. Maybe I can't love her enough to prevent her from seeing herself as not good enough. Maybe society's message of unattainable model perfection is too powerful; maybe my little girl can't escape that unscathed.

But I know I have a power of my own. The way she looks at me as if the sun and moon rise because of me is one of the scariest things I've ever experienced. How easy it would be to abuse that power, to hurt my little girl, and I'm sure I have hurt her unintentionally. But as long as I am her daddy, I vow to use my power for good, to give her unconditional love that can maybe lessen the impact of the inevitable, if it can't stop it.

And even if that doesn't work, she will always have a hug and kiss waiting for her because she's my Sweetie Girl. Society can't take that away from us.

## The Opportunities of Dinner Together

While out to dinner the other night, I saw a couple sitting with their two kids, who were about ten and twelve years old. Each child pulled out a device and put headphones on. What kind of message does that send about family time and talking together?

I can talk a good game about how much screen time kids should have, but I know our kids play with iTouches, spend time on computers, and watch TV more than they should (whatever that means). Screens are a part of our lives and I'm not trying to rid our lives of them. But seeing that family got me thinking about when they're appropriate.

While talking with Gem about it, I realized what worries me. Our family had recently had some fascinating discussions at the breakfast/dinner table. We'd had a great talk with our kids about making sure they let us know about any pain they were feeling (our daughter had an appendectomy recently). We'd also talked about what to do when someone is sitting shiva (the wife of someone in my office recently died). In fact, we'd even had a great discussion about school that ended up leading us to send them to a different school because they were so unhappy at the last one.

The way I see it, screens aren't inherently bad. But screens keep us from interacting with each other. Anytime we watch dinner in front of the TV, we lose the chance for a conversation. Anytime someone uses a phone or device at the table, he or she isn't present with the family.

Certainly once in a while, having dinner in front of a good movie, cuddled on the couch, is lovely. But I think about what eating together means to our family, and what would happen if we didn't have this time. When we sit down at the table we don't plan the discussion, but we all know it's a chance to share what's been going on with us—good or bad. I can talk about a big project at work. Gem can tell us about a workshop she ran that day. The kids can tell us something that happened during their days at school. But the reactions and the questions are always the best part. I love seeing where the conversation goes. Some nights it's just an interesting conversation. And some nights, Gem and I find ourselves with the chance to remind our children of something very important. Sometimes it's about sex or drugs or drinking. Sometimes it's about what it means to be good friend, or how to deal with problems. Sometimes it's about my past and how different things are for me now. It's never what we expected, but always of value.

A screen prevents all of this from happening. I hope that as our kids get older, things will happen to them during the day and they'll think, "Oh, I can talk about this at dinner." If it works out like that, both Gem and I will be tremendously excited.

What happens at dinner is always better than what happens on any screen.

## Boys and Men

I'm grateful for the fact that as my children get older, they still look to me as a role model—my son, in particular. Ten years old, he watches me going through my routine the way he used to watch me when he was a toddler. Except now, he loves watching me shave.

I've always hated shaving, and mostly try to avoid it if I can. But recently I found some products—oil, shaving cream, and aftershave lotion—that helped change the experience for the better.

They have also made it even more interesting to Lucas, as well.

It still feels strange to be stared it, to have someone look at me as if I'm the be all and end all (though I know that won't last much longer). But now I have more parenting years under my belt and am better prepared to be there for Lucas in ways that were more challenging when I (and he) was younger.

When I put the oil on my face, he watches as if this is the most interesting TV show he's seen all year. He loves how I use a shaving brush, how I get it wet and then put the shaving cream on and brush it on my face. He even loves when I rinse the brush, and watches the cream wash out of it.

I think his favorite part is the actual shaving, though. The way I transform right in front of his eyes. The way the blade slides along my skin, removing the white cream on my face and neck. He finds it utterly fascinating.

Last week, Lucas said to me, "It's a good thing I get to watch you, Daddy. Then I'll be ready when it's my turn."

And that's what is amazing about this. I'm his role model. He's known on some level all along that we are the same sex, that who I am now is very similar to who he will be when he grows up. He watches me, studying for the invisible test of adulthood, looking for answers to help him as he matures.

I still wonder: What does he think about while he watches? Am I doing enough for him? Enabling him to feel the strong connection I feel with him? I do know that I've come to look forward to his questions, to his staring at me. I hope he finds the answers he needs and sees what he needs to see.

I want to be his male role model, and hope that his watching me makes the transition to manhood a bit easier for him.

## Boundary and Responsibility

There aren't many things Gem and I disagree on (fortunately), but we do differ on a few issues. For example, Gem believes that our okapis don't need much privacy. If they want to have time alone, that's fine. But she wants to know pretty much everything they're doing. This is due partly to her general sense of nosiness (sorry, Sweetie). But it's also due largely to her belief that we're responsible for our children and thus need to know what they're doing, where they're going, who they're with, etc.

I feel that if they don't want us to know, then we don't need to know. It's a boundary issue. I believe boundaries are extremely important, and I want our kids to be able to create strong ones, since I wasn't able to have them when I was a kid.

In fact, my parents never inquired about my life. We had a deal: if I did my homework and didn't have trouble in school, they wouldn't ask me about it at all. And they didn't. They didn't know about the work I did or the tests or papers I had. When I was a kid, this seemed like a great deal. Looking back as a parent, I wonder what they were thinking. Because this isn't really a boundary issue (even if it feels like one to me).

How am I supposed to teach my children about being responsible if I don't know what homework they have or what tests or papers are due? How are Gem and I supposed to help them with any struggles if we haven't created an environment in which they feel comfortable talking to us? There's a big difference between being alone and doing it on your own. Our twins can do things on their own, but I don't want my okapis to ever feel alone, to ever feel they have to do it all alone.

My wife understands this on a fairly primal level. She inquires because she wants them to know we're paying attention and are interested in what goes on in their lives. And also because we need to know what they're doing in order to keep them healthy. When they come home from a day with the grandparents, she always asks what they ate, what they did, etc. Honestly, it doesn't occur to me to ask. They're home safe and sound and that's all that matters to me. She arranged all of their play dates when they were young, and almost always got to know the parents before scheduling one, just to make sure she was comfortable with the people who would be taking care of our children for a couple of hours. Makes perfect sense to me, but I wouldn't have thought of it.

She's like this in the virtual world as well. When our kids first started using the Internet, we paid attention to the websites they were visiting and made them get permission from us before they went to a new one. When we helped our kids create their own email addresses to email with family and friends and some teachers, Gem would periodically check their email. Sometimes with them and sometimes without. She told them we would be doing this.

Does that cross a boundary? Absolutely! It makes my stomach knot up just thinking about it. But is it wrong? I don't think so. Our okapis aren't even teenagers yet. They need our protection and supervision.

The real challenge will come when our little okapis are teenagers. When they have their own Snapchat and Twitter and Facebook accounts and block us from seeing what's on them, what will we do? When they have their own email addresses and we don't have the passwords, how will we handle it? As they get older, more and more of their lives will become private, and we will need to respect their boundaries while still protecting them and being there for them when they need us. It's a delicate balance.

We can only hope the foundation we've been laying for all of these years supports them, and our family together, in the way we planned.

## I Got My Own Calvin

The story started many years ago (but I'll try to control myself and keep it relatively short). When she was about five or six years old, my daughter had trouble going to sleep at night, so we let her take her iPod nano to bed with her. It had no Internet connection or texting capabilities—just music. Relaxing music really made a difference for her when it came time to calm down and get some sleep.

When my twins got iPod Touches, they started taking those to bed for music. Again, it wasn't a big deal because they didn't use the devices for texting much, and they didn't have social media yet.

But then teenagerhood hit.

Now I have two fourteen-year-olds (someone is usually pretty moody, heh heh). They started taking their iPhones to bed with them for the music. And now they have social media, and friends to socialize with. Were they really obeying our rules and not communicating with friends? Not surfing the net at night? Neither my wife nor I really believed that. Plus, we knew it wasn't healthy to take a screen to bed. Something had to change.

But I knew how important having music to go to bed with meant to them (because it means so much to me as well), and didn't want to take that away without an alternative.

At one point I cut them off from the Wi-Fi, but since they still had 3G service, that only served to increase our data overages. I needed a better answer.

I looked into Bluetooth speakers, so they could keep their phones outside their room but still hear the music. But what if they wanted to change the music? They'd have to get out of bed. That didn't seem like such a good idea either.

Finally, I looked into the Echo Dot from Amazon. The Echo Dot is a small hockey-puck-like speaker that responds (most of the time) to voice commands with Alexa. They could access all sorts of music just by asking Alexa to play it—plus, they could connect it to their headphones.

I was pretty proud of myself for coming up with this solution. So proud, in fact, that I bought one for each of them and one for the kitchen, since Amazon had a Black Friday sale going on.

My kids, shockingly, were nowhere near as excited as I was. My son didn't take it in stride but dealt with it.

My daughter decided to not handle it as well. It's possible things might have been thrown; maybe a hanger was bent out of shape and thrown against the door; she may have mentioned to my wife that she was trying to figure out a way to break poor little Alexa into pieces to get back at me. Talk about an innocent bystander!

There was a lot of crying about the cruelty of Daddy, and how I was ruining her life or something. It was hard to tell through the crying. Finally, she seemed to calm down, and my wife I went downstairs to watch some Netflix.

But within a few minutes, our lovely daughter left her room, and I went upstairs to see what suspicious trouble she was trying to get herself into. Instead of trouble, I found her drinking water from the faucet. I stood and watched for a moment, and then she walked right by me, mumbled something, and returned to her room.

It took a moment for my echoic memory to replay what she had said.

"I'm rehydrating so I can cry some more."

Man, it's a good thing I hadn't heard it right away because I would've laughed right in her face, which would not have helped the situation. I still love that moment now.

The reason I enjoy it so is because I didn't experience disrespect or teenager attitude. Instead, I heard a sassy comment and felt, well, pride. My girl used her smart mouth and her anger toward me in a creative way to try to make me feel guilty (which she knows almost never works on me anyway).

I mean, that's a top-five sassy comment, my friends. How could I have not felt proud? The truth is, I'd always wanted a child like Calvin from Calvin and Hobbes, and this was my dream coming true.

It's funny, because now when we talk about it, she says, "When I said that, I didn't realize it would become part of my legacy."

As crazy as being a teenager makes that girl, how can I not love her!

## Holding On until She Lets Go

I once drove up to Connecticut to watch my Sweetie Girl perform in a musical. But instead of going home afterwards, I treated myself and booked a B&B so I could spend a few hours with her.

Now, some parents of thirteen-year-olds complain about how their kids don't really talk or answer questions, but I barely got to say anything at all over the four hours we spent together. My lovely daughter told me every single detail about the musical and her friends and the scenery and the audio and sound effects and the actors and their issues and concerns and strengths and weaknesses and which songs were her favorite and which performances were the best and all of the melodrama and so much more.

Periodically, I would marvel that this was her first time at sleepaway camp, and while she genuinely claimed to miss Gem and me, you wouldn't have been able to tell. She had made new friends and given her entire being to this musical, with rehearsals frequently taking up five to six hours of her day every day.

And not once did she complain. Not once did she say it wasn't worth it. She LOVED it. I mean, this girl of mine L O V E D every moment. What had once been an interest was now a burning passion: being on stage and performing. It's incredible how much she's like her daddy in that way, but so much more talented, thankfully.

But what was most amazing was that after the show, she ran to me and gave me a hug. When we walked outside, she held my hand. She gave me a big hug and kiss when I left. At thirteen years old, she wasn't embarrassed by affection with her daddy.

Every time it happens, I wonder if it will be the last time. Could this be the last time she holds my hand in public? Or the last time she runs up to give me a hug?

But I'm not being pessimistic or negative. No, I'm trying to savor every moment. My little girl is not so little anymore. She's a full-fledged teenager. The fact that she still holds my hand could easily be construed as a miracle.

And it feels that way every time. I don't (really) care that she's now taller than I am, or that she texts her friends constantly and barely responds to my messages. When my daughter wants to hold my hand when we're walking together, I thank my lucky stars and hold on until she wants to let go. When she runs up to me, I brace myself to catch her as best I can and swing her around. I can't do it quite like I did when she was five, but good enough for government work, and for her to know I love her.

And honestly, those big hugs are one of my favorite parts of being a daddy. Hugs are a moment in time when I can feel her love, when I am 100 percent in the present, when my past is just a faraway spot in my rearview mirror. It's a moment where her love for me, her Daddy, and my love for my Sweetie Girl swirl together in a powerful vortex that makes us both feel better, feel special.

It's amazing to watch my children grow up and see how independent they're becoming, and how they're learning to handle new situations. This growing independence makes it even more important for Gem and me to celebrate, embrace, and bask in the moments when they show us affection and love just as freely as they did when they were younger.

As I was leaving to head to the B&B, I thanked Dorit for such a special day and she smiled at me, that beautiful smile that reminds me so much of her mother's, and she thanked me for such a special day. A day of driving and eating and talking. And of hugs and holding hands and reminding each other we love each other. And of musicals, of course.

I will hold on to this day as long as I can, and that feeling we had together. These are the days that make being a parent the most amazing job in the world.

## Yes, My Okapis Will Have Sex and Drink

It appears we are living in denial. According to a 2016 study conducted by the University of Michigan, only 10 percent of parents believe their teenagers have had any alcohol to drink in the last year, and only 5 percent believe their teens have used marijuana in the last year. In fact, a 2016 study by Monitoring the Future revealed that 52 percent of tenth graders say they drank alcohol in the last year, and 28 percent say the same about marijuana. This means over half of all tenth graders are drinking. There is a serious disconnect here. Not surprisingly, 40 percent of parents believe other teenagers are more likely to drink or smoke marijuana than their own.

The problem isn't that there are so many teenagers drinking and smoking. The problem is the fact that their parents aren't aware of it, that this issue has become so taboo that it's talked about almost as much as sex—which is to say very rarely.

If there's anything I've learned about parenting it's that my Okapis never—repeat, NEVER—get anything the first time I tell them. For example, I've been telling my kids to put their towels away after showering for several years and still have to remind them. There are so many things I have to tell them over and over and over and over and over again. Why would I believe that anything would be different in regards to alcohol, drugs, and even sex?

The reality is that nothing is different—except for how we as parents feel about it. We want to teach them manners and to be responsible, so we remind them to say thank you and to pick up that damn towel and put it away! And we want to teach them to be safe, so we've been talking about sex, drugs, and alcohol for years as well.

There's "the sex talk" and "the drug talk," but if we'd only talked to our children about sex or drugs and alcohol once, during "the talk," we would have an enormous problem now (they're fifteen). What if we'd had "the talk" too early? Or even worse, as is more likely the case, too late? If we hadn't talked about it, we would have sent the message that it wasn't something we discussed, which meant they would have been forced to learn about it through something else (read Internet) or someone else (read a friend already drinking, smoking, and/or having sex). Frankly, there's no one I would rather our kids turn to than me (or my wife) to learn about these things. That's why we frequently have discussions about it, and when it does come up in a TV show or in a conversation with one of their friends, we talk about it again so they know how we feel about it and that we want them to come to us with questions.

I could never talk to my parents about this stuff. My parents almost never drank and were against drugs, and I did absorb that. But I was uncomfortable around anyone who drank in high school and spent years in college afraid I was an alcoholic without ever having had a beer or much to drink because I was so scared of it, scared of what it could do to me. I'd really like my kids to have a healthier perspective on drinking.

My wife, on the other hand, is comfortable drinking, and enjoys it. For Shabbat, we open up a couple of bottles of wine and share them among our extended family. It's a fun and festive affair. Our okapis see their family drink, see that it's fun, but no one gets drunk or sick or loud or obnoxious, etc. We can already tell that Lucas will probably be more like me while Dorit will be more like her mother.

The fact is, my lovely little okapis are going to drink. They're going to have sex. They're probably going to try drugs of some sort. I just hope they know we are there for them with any questions or problems they have. And I really hope they remember to be safe and responsible. That's what we've been talking about for all these years.

And please remember that just because my kids will probably drink or try drugs doesn't mean yours won't.

# Chapter Eight

# When Do We Find Out Our Grade?

*One of the most challenging and rarely talked about aspects of parenting is that we really have no idea how well we're doing. And we won't find out how well we did as parents until our children are grown up and it's too late to do anything about it. There's a leap of faith required, and it can be unsettling. But there are some ways we can assess ourselves while our kids are still kids. We just have to look out for them.*

## Saving a Sparrow

Lucas and I were standing by the front door. Out of nowhere, he said, "Remember when we saved that bird?"

"I do."

"That was pretty cool."

"It really was, wasn't it?"

It always makes me feel good when one of my kids remembers fondly something we did together.

When our kids were about five years old, Gem and Dorit had gone out and Lucas and I were having quality Daddy-Son time on a weekend morning. It was a cold, wintry day, and when I looked outside, I caught sight of something on the ground on our porch. I went out to inspect it more closely and realized it was a sparrow.

It looked almost frozen, as if it hadn't found a warm place to sleep through the night and was so chilled it could no longer move.

For several minutes, Lucas and I watched it through the door, but I soon knew something was really wrong. So I went back outside and lifted the bird gently into a basket full of blankets, which I left on the porch.

Lucas and I watched some more, but even after more time passed, our little sparrow didn't move or make any progress. That's when I brought it inside.

I placed the basket on the stairs, and somehow Lucas and I got distracted by something. By the time we returned, our little sparrow seemed to be feeling much better. Well, maybe it was feeling too good.

It was perched on the basket, and as I approached it, instead of thanking us for our efforts to save it, our little sparrow flew upstairs. And I started to see how terribly wrong this all could go. Yeah, let's bring a sickly little bird into our home, where it can wreak havoc. It's possible I could've thought it through a tad more.

Lucas and I ran upstairs after it and found it perched atop the curtains in his room. Honestly, the thing I was most worried about was that it would poop. How the heck would I explain that to Gem when she got home? "Hi, Sweetie, we saved a bird today (and got poop all over the kids' room, by the way)."

Thankfully, that didn't happen. Our recovering bird probably hadn't eaten in a long time and spared us that … ummm … experience.

But even so, it was quite frustrating trying to shoo the bird back downstairs without hurting it or scaring it too badly, since we knew it was probably still pretty fragile.

Finally, we urged it back downstairs and it landed on the only place it was already familiar with, the basket, and we took the basket outside and let our little patient fly away. Lucas and I shared a look, impressed with ourselves. We had actually saved a bird that day. What a great feeling!

I remember wondering a day or two later, when I didn't see any dead sparrows on our property, if our little sparrow had made it. Looking back now, I realize this is often what parenting feels like. We do so much for our kids, but we just don't know how it will all play out. I'd hate to wake up in ten years and find out I'd been doing something unintentionally that really screwed up my kids.

But in moments like these, when one of my children reminds me of a special experience we shared, I can see a little of the positive impact I've had on their lives. It's pretty nice feeling.

## Comforting Elmo

"Did I tell you what Dorit did today during nebby?" Gem asked me.

"I don't think so." "Nebby" is what we call nebulizing. When our twins were young, we had to nebulize them every night to prevent asthma from developing and to decrease the congestion in their pulmonary systems.

"She was holding her Elmo in a blanket and patting him on the back, saying, 'It's okay, Elmo. It's okay. It's almost over and then you'll feel better. You feel better, right?'"

Tears welled up in her eyes as well as in mine, and we couldn't say anything at all for a moment. I could picture my little girl doing that, could hear her voice in my head.

"That little girl has been through so much." My voice sounded hoarse, cracked, and Gem looked as if she hadn't heard me.

"I know. I know," she said, her voice sounding far away.

Our twins were born almost two and a half months early. Dorit weighed only three pounds. She had trouble breathing and needed a ventilator for a couple of days until she could breathe well enough on her own. They both spent one month in the hospital before we could take them home with us.

Two months after she was born and only four weeks after she came home from the hospital, Dorit required laser surgery on both of her eyes to prevent her retinas from becoming detached. It was challenging waiting all morning for the surgery to start. She was starving and thirsty from not being allowed to eat or drink anything—as if the surgery itself wasn't torture enough. Afterwards, my little girl's face was swollen, and she clearly didn't feel well. But she had no idea what was happening. I wanted so badly to help, but there was nothing I could do for her. Gem and I comforted ourselves by telling each other she wouldn't remember any of this. If it had to happen, now was the best time, since she wouldn't have any knowledge of it as she got older.

A few months later we found this thing on her belly. Day after day this thing grew. We took her to a specialist and learned she needed to have it removed, as it could become cancerous. I'll never forget pinning her down to prevent her from jerking around while trying to soothe her with my voice. Her screams and cries broke my heart. When it was over, my ears echoed the way they do after a rock concert. All of this while my face was only inches away from the surgical tool slicing the growth off her belly. As she grows, her scar grows with her, a constant reminder of that traumatic day. I keep hoping it will disappear, so I can pretend she never had to go through that.

Shortly thereafter, Gem and I found out that while the eye surgery had saved Dorit from going blind, it wasn't enough. Her brain wasn't paying attention to the signals one of her eyes was sending. If this continued for too long, she would lose her sight completely in that eye. The solution: she had to wear a patch over her good eye for an hour a day to strengthen the weaker eye.

The hour she wore the patch quickly became the worst hour of the day for all of us. She would rip it off as soon as we turned away, and we'd have to put on a new one. Then we noticed that every time she ripped it off, she was ripping out her eyebrow hair as well. The patch the doctor had recommended was essentially a bandage; it stuck to her face with adhesive. Before I knew it, I found myself pinning her down once again just to put the damn patch on her. If we put the patch on her, we were clearly causing her pain. If we didn't put the patch on her, we would allow her to go blind. We chose the lesser of two evils and hated ourselves for hurting her so much.

Then the doctor said she needed to wear the patch for six hours a day because her eye was getting even worse. Getting Dorit to wear that sticky patch for most of the day was a horrific struggle. She would rip it off, we would put it back on, and she would rip it off again. Within a day or two, she developed an irritation over her eye from ripping the patch off so much. Fortunately, I found better patches online, from a site called Patch Pals (www.patchpals.com). These patches fit over Dorit's glasses, and they had designs on them. We bought her one with a panda and one with a helicopter.

They changed everything. She thought they were adorable, she got to choose which one she wanted, and if she took her glasses off, it was easy and painless to put them back on. All of a sudden six hours a day was relatively easy—which worked out well because when we went back to the doctor, he said he wanted her to start wearing the patch eight hours a day. As well, he told us she would have to wear it eight hours a day for about one year, and would then have to wear it for a significant part of the day until she was six or seven years old.

During this time, we also found out that both of our children have something called reactive airway disease, which is essentially the precursor to asthma. Both of our children's air passages are smaller than they should be (primarily because they were born so prematurely), and when they get colds, the mucous restricts air flow and they have difficulty breathing. To prevent this from happening, they have to be nebulized every night with a preventative medicine—and if they have a cold or are coughing, with an additional medicine as well.

The first three years of our Dorit's life was a sometimes agonizing triathlon of surgeries, patches, and nebulization; three years of consoling ourselves by saying she wouldn't remember what she had been through, that it probably hurt us more than it hurt her. But when our little girl comforted her Elmo, mimicking the way we'd comforted her through all that she'd endured, our hearts broke. She did remember. Maybe not all of it, maybe not everything, but too much. And as much as I want to, I can't do anything to change that.

But I have to remind myself that she was able to comfort Elmo because she experienced our comfort, our love, and it helped her. When I see her running around or intently watching a video or reading a book, I remember that my little girl doesn't have cancer, she can breathe well, and she can see. It could've been so much worse. Everything we did, we did to save her from something even worse.

Maybe she comforted Elmo not because we failed, but because we succeeded.

## No One Keeps Score in Parenting

My wife and I met with a school counselor. Dorit had been having trouble going to sleep at night because she was so stressed—stressed about all of the schoolwork and about whether people (teachers, us) would still like her if she didn't continue to excel.

I think there were a number of factors contributing to her stress. Our okapis had just entered third grade, which was certainly harder than second, with more responsibilities, more homework. They had also just started Hebrew school two days a week, and that was another setting where Dorit wasn't comfortable, where things were completely new and challenging. In addition, my little girl is incredibly sensitive and connected to her emotions, and often they can overwhelm her.

We talked with her about all of this. Since she's one of the more emotionally intelligent people we know, we tried to help her write and draw her feelings, to express them, and that helped a little. We'd ask her to tell us the worst that could happen, and we'd tell her that if she completely and utterly failed a test or messed up her homework or whatever, we would still love her and give her a hug. Nothing in the world would change that. We tried to change her bedtime routine so she didn't have as much time to get anxious about going to sleep. Whatever helped didn't seem to help for more than a night or two, sadly. So we figured that before her lack of sleep started to affect her at school, we should talk to someone.

We met with George, and he just radiated genuineness and empathy. We sat down and talked, and before long I had tears in my eyes as I described the struggles my little girl was having. I'd had struggles when I was a kid but no one to help me. I'd been put in therapy when I was nine—my little girl would be nine in two months. I didn't want to do that to her, but I also didn't want to ignore her struggles, pretend they would just magically get better on their own. I felt frozen by these two polar-opposite approaches, neither of which I wanted to choose for Dorit.

But talking to George really helped. He let us know that kids really do seem to have more stress than before—especially since third graders take the New York State standardized test for the first time. And he gave us a couple of suggestions, new things to try. He also told us we were doing a great job, raising our children in a way that allowed them to experience and express their emotions. We walked out of there feeling much better.

In sports, it's easy to know when you're doing well—you score a goal, hit a home run, win the game. At work we have performance evaluations. You can get three stars in Angry Birds. In so many areas of our lives, there are quantifiable ways to determine whether we're doing well, or improving. Not with parenting. But George gave us some rare feedback on how we were doing as parents, and it was a little boost to our depleted confidence.

I later had the idea of giving Dorit a Calvin and Hobbes comic book to read before bed because it would make her laugh, lighten her mind. And she did in fact start falling asleep more easily.

But I also wonder if maybe she started falling asleep more easily because Gem and I were suddenly less stressed out about our parenting skills after our meeting with George.

## Oh But Those Moments

We are in full-fledged teenage mode in our house now. So much is different.

Gone are the days when we cuddled.
  Gone are the days when we sat on the rug and played together.
  Gone are the days when they were willing to watch a movie or TV show because we suggested it.
  Gone are the days when I could pick them both up and hold them.
  Gone are the days when we would tuck them into bed.

Now we have moodiness and agitation and need for alone time and addiction to iPhones and chatting with friends and friends of friends and friends of friends of friends.
  Now we hear "No" and "Why" much more than we'd like.
  Now they want friends over because they're more fun than we are.
  Now our lives are more exhausting because our kids are more challenging than ever before.
  Now there are moments of pure selfishness and thoughtlessness that are hard not to take personally even though we know it isn't personal.
  Now we have moments when we wonder where we went wrong.
  Now we're lucky if we sometimes get a hug and kiss before they go to bed.
  Now we have less time together because our teenagers go to bed later.

But I'll tell you …
  When the moment is right, when the sun and moon are aligned properly and the ocean tides are in rhythm and the hormones release our children from their hold …
  These moments, moments of fascinating conversation and extraordinary insight into who these young people are and who they are becoming, they are the most delicious moments of my life.

I recently had three of those moments in a huge bonus day. It started when I came home and my daughter ran into my arms and gave me a huge hug and kiss. What a wonderful way to come home from work!

Later, my son and I were talking about Broadway musicals and he expressed concern that one of the shows we were considering seeing would trigger issues from my past. My fourteen-year-old son, consumed with crazy hormones, was still able to be concerned about me, and wanted to make sure I could still have a good time when we went to the theater. That led us to an interesting discussion about what is appropriate and what is offensive and where my lines are and where his are. How amazing to not only experience my son's compassion, and hear him express that compassion so articulately, but also to listen to him share his thoughts and ideas and perspective in a fascinating way that left me thinking about what he'd said.

Finally, that night I went to say good night to my daughter and we ended up sharing some music with each other. I played her Nina Simone's "Be My Husband," and then she played a song from *Dear Evan Hansen*, the Broadway show my son was talking about earlier. Then I shared another version of "Be My Husband," which appeared in *The Magicians* (a show she's obsessed with), and she shared a song from a new Broadway show starring Ani DiFranco (she knows I've always liked her). There's something about sharing music that is so wonderful. Music means so much to both of us (as she likes to joke, it's all my fault), and what she's listening to, what's affecting her, gives me insight into how she's feeling. By sharing what we're listening to, we're sharing an intimate part of ourselves with each other, and it feels special.

Now, I might go days without any of these moments, which is one of the biggest challenges of parenting two teenagers. But I cherish them when they come. And I hold on to them as long as I can.

They remind me that maybe Gem and I are doing okay as parents after all. They remind me that being a parent is wonderful. They remind me of how far we've come.

# Conclusion

I hope you enjoyed these snapshots of my life as a man trying to become a daddy while working away from home full-time. I hope they helped you understand that how we fathers feel when our children are born—the lack of confidence, the nervousness, the unfamiliarity with all of the parenting tasks—it really doesn't last long and doesn't have any long-term impact.

When my kids were born, they spent four weeks in the neonatal intensive care unit. Four weeks away from each other in separate isolettes. I remember being so worried about how detrimental this would be to their special twin bond. Would it still develop? Would they have a good relationship? Of course, four weeks apart is nothing compared to fifteen years of being together, and their relationship is more adorable and powerful than I ever thought it could be. They even miss each other when one goes to school and the other is sick.

The same logic applies to us new fathers. Those first couple of months, I was so worried about my lack of connection with my children. I worried about all of the mistakes I was making, the struggles I was having, the doubts I was experiencing. Even though these things seemed SO important at the time, they didn't matter after a while. Again, two months is nothing compared to fifteen years.

Now, I have something very special with my children. We are Los Tres Amigos, and we'll continue to grow together and bond. As they get older things change; what we did to bond when they were toddlers doesn't really work anymore. But we keep coming up with new ways to spend time together and have fun. I believe this is a result of the foundation we created—even while I was so worried about my lack of connection to them. A strong foundation allows a relationship to adjust and grow over time to better meet each person's needs.

Hopefully, these snapshots remind you of what's so easy to forget as a parent in the chaos of our lives. We love them. They love us. The rest of our daily craziness matters a little bit less when we have a home, a place where love ties us together, even when we're not physically next to each other.

At the end of the day, when my children lay their heads on their pillows to go to sleep, all that matters is that they know they are loved and accepted completely and unconditionally.

Because when you have a baseline of love, acceptance, and support, everything in the chaos of life is easier to manage.